HE SAID *then* SHE SAID

Helping Jewish-Gentile Couples Find Spiritual Harmony

by Tuvya Zaretsky

JEWS FOR JESUS®

San Francisco, CA

He Said . . . Then She Said: Helping Jewish-Gentile Couples Find Spiritual Harmony
By Tuvya Zaretsky
Edited by Ruth Rosen

JEWS FOR JESUS®

Cover design: Paige Saunders
Inside design: David Yapp

For more information, including reprint permission, contact:
Jews for Jesus
60 Haight Street
San Francisco, CA 94102
USA

jewsforjesus.org
jfj@jewsforjesus.org

ISBN-10: 1-881022-07-2
ISBN-13: 978-1-881022-07-7

Contents

Introduction

Mark was dying of abdominal cancer. His girlfriend, Susan, was a Christian who'd wandered from her relationship with the Lord. Now she wanted desperately to help her boyfriend find eternal life in Jesus. And Mark? He was the son of Holocaust survivors; he'd been raised in the practices of Orthodox Judaism, but had discontinued them as an adult. He wasn't the least bit interested in Jesus. He just wanted to marry Susan before he died.

Susan contacted me at the Jews for Jesus office. Could I come and help her tell Mark about the Savior? Of course I could! I asked Susan to let Mark know that I am a Jew who believes in Jesus. That was only fair to him.

I'll never forget our first meeting. Mark stood with difficulty, his illness painfully obvious. Without any greeting, he lifted his finger to point at me as he announced, "I will never believe like you!"

Susan was confused. "Why is he so angry? What did I do?"

Mark was frustrated. "Why does she put Jesus between us when I love her and all I want to do is marry her?"

Mark and Susan are one of the couples to whom I have dedicated this book. Their situation was complicated, yet they represent an ever-growing opportunity for ministry among a particular group of people: Jewish-Gentile couples.

A Bit of Background

Why are there so many opportunities to share the gospel with Jewish people today? The answer to that is tied to changes within the Jewish community. Understanding those changes will help you get a handle on the opportunities.

In 1990 I was reading *Moment* magazine, a popular cultural observer of Jewish people worldwide. One article reported that 63 percent of American Jewish people were "disaffiliated" from any Jewish institution. Jews were flocking away from synagogue, and nearly two-thirds didn't even read a Jewish periodical or pay attention to literature about Jewish concerns. The Jewish birthrate had dropped to 1.8 per couple, meaning that the Jewish population was decreasing.

At the same time, intermarriage had spiked. 52 percent of all Jews who married since 1985 had married Gentiles. American Jewish leaders regarded that as a clear danger to the survival of the Jewish people. Studies and task forces were mobilized to address what was then viewed as a catastrophic crisis.

Many Jewish-Gentile couples wanted advice about the challenges they faced but did not find what they were looking for from Jewish community leaders—so they began searching elsewhere. By 1995, more Jewish-Gentile couples were calling our Jews for Jesus office in Southern California, asking for help.

One study claims that the divorce rate among Jewish-Gentile couples is approximately double that of Jewish-Jewish couples.

Then, in 1998, I received a telephone call that changed the direction of my ministry with Jews for Jesus.

The caller represented a group of four Jewish-Gentile couples. They all had young children and questions about how to raise them. And though the Jewish partners were reluctant to hear from Jewish believers in Jesus, they were motivated by the intensity of the challenges and tensions they were experiencing. They were serious about wanting to strengthen their marriages and hoped we might help them find some sort of common ground despite their religious differences.

Sociologists and psychologists report that interfaith couples experience more threats to their marital stability than do same-faith couples. One study claims that the divorce rate among Jewish-Gentile couples is approximately double that of Jewish-Jewish couples. In fact, one study not only claimed "mixed-faith marriages significantly increase the rate of disillusion," but also that "couples with no religious affiliation also have fairly high rates of disillusion."[1]

Meeting a Need

The couples that wanted to meet with me didn't know these statistics—they just knew they were facing challenges they could not afford to ignore. Their love for one another had opened them to seek help. They had questions about how to be fair in giving their children religious advice. Where could they find a community that would make them welcome without trying to change either of them?

They had received a lot of advice from relatives, religious leaders and well-meaning friends—to no avail. So, instead of giving advice, I began by asking them to tell me about their challenges. And I listened to their answers.

Good, focused listening builds the kind of trust that opens doors to ministry.

Listening does not require us either to judge or affirm what we hear. Listening that merely takes in what others say for the purpose of understanding them is a first step in developing trust. That trust can lead to meaningful conversations where, ultimately, we might be able to help people understand their deepest spiritual need.

So I listened as these couples described their frustrations, anger and impatience with each other—and even their despair bordering on hopelessness.

I heard some often-repeated themes. Gentile Christian partners didn't want to compromise their commitment to Jesus; Jewish partners recoiled at the thought of anything that might threaten their Jewish identity, or the survival of the Jewish people. Partners seemed unable to understand something so basic as one another's identity, yet they wanted intimacy right down to their souls. I don't remember anyone using the term "spiritual harmony," but I've found that phrase describes what people want, but don't know how to achieve.

I realized that I had much to learn in order to serve these couples effectively, so I pursued a doctor of missiology in the Division of Intercultural Studies at Western Seminary. What I learned revolutionized my approach to Jewish-Gentile couples.

In 2004, I interviewed 52 couples who were willing to take part in an original social research study.[2] I asked them to describe the challenges they faced. These are the top five that surfaced during that study:

1. Confusion over identity
2. Tension over religious differences
3. Disagreements over life-cycle celebrations
4. Challenges to family harmony
5. Discord over training children

You will get the benefit of all the insights provided by the couples who spoke candidly with me, including some of their stories. (I've changed their names to protect their privacy.) I continue learning from each couple I meet (and so will you). You will need to ask the couples you meet about their own personal challenges, but since many are likely to bring up some of the challenges I'm sharing with you, you will have a good head start on understanding their concerns.

The Purpose of This Workbook

Maybe you picked up this workbook to help you reach specific couples you already know and care for. Or maybe you want to become better equipped to share the gospel with Jewish people, who are often overlooked when it comes to evangelism. Most of what you'll discover about ministry to Jewish-Gentile couples will help you share your faith with Jewish people in general.

In any case, I hope you are reading this because you believe the gospel is the only hope of finding peace with God, and that peace with God is the key to people finding peace with one another.[3] The gospel transforms lives. Through Jesus we receive God's forgiveness and find He has the power to heal relationships that are damaged by our sin and selfishness. So, how do you introduce that wonderful message to a couple like Mark and Susan? That's what you're about to find out.

You will learn about sensitivities that act as roadblocks between Jewish-Gentile couples. As you help them navigate past these sensitivities, you'll be able to facilitate meaningful, spiritual discussions. You'll learn to ask meaningful questions and recognize natural connecting points to the gospel as they arise.

Those connecting points are important because many Jewish-Gentile couples are not in touch with their spiritual needs; they just know that their differences are confusing and painful. Most do not recognize that the root of interpersonal conflicts is the broken relationships between people and God. And that's not something people will grasp just because we show them chapter and verse in the Bible.

While God's Word is powerful to change lives—if people don't know that it's relevant to them personally, they don't read it. For example, a couple might be interested to see what the Bible says about intermarriage long before they are interested in how to have their sins forgiven . . . especially if they don't really know what sin is.

So while we have spiritual answers, the couples you encounter might not yet be asking questions that invite those answers. But don't worry; many things that will naturally come up in conversation can serve as springboards to those deeper questions.

Please note: this workbook is not an evangelistic resource for Christians to hand to Jewish seekers. It's a resource for Christians who want to help Jewish-Gentile couples find spiritual harmony.

What You'll Need

You'll need to develop a patient and listening ear if you don't already have one. As you listen, you'll learn to ask the right questions. As you respond to complex people and situations with humility, love, kindness and clarity, you'll find yourself guiding discussions that won't pressure people, but present opportunities for them to see new possibilities.

You'll need to be patient in building relationships. Part of that is being a good listener and part is your own transparency. When meeting with Jewish-Gentile couples, I am candid about my identity as a Jew for Jesus from the start. Conversation that is straight up without a whiff of manipulation is crucial in building trust—and trust helps clear the path to go forward into those places that many find uncomfortable.

You'll need to wait for and recognize opportunities for spiritual conversations. I am convinced that the power of the gospel is the only way for people to have a relationship with the God of

Abraham, Isaac and Jacob, no matter their ethnicity or cultural background. As Jesus Himself put it, "I am the way, the truth, and the life. No one comes to the Father except through Me" (John 14:6). I guess today we could say He is the PIN to the ATM or the password to log into the account.

However—and this is important—the fact that I openly believe this does not mean I start the conversation by telling a couple why they need to believe the gospel. You should not feel it necessary to begin the conversation that way either.

I find it helpful to begin with the attitude that says, "You don't really know me and I really don't know you. Over time, we can understand each other better." And as these couples and I get to know each other, we begin to create a solid ground of trust where we can eventually unearth spiritual treasure together.

As these couples and I get to know each other, we begin to create a solid ground of trust where we can eventually unearth spiritual treasure together.

You'll need to trust God and remember that while we serve Him by serving other people, He's the only one who can change hearts and bring about the spiritual harmony these couples need.

I've learned a lot from people like Mark and Susan. And here's what I didn't tell you when I first mentioned their story. Though he insisted at the outset, "I will never believe like you!" as though determined not to hear anything about Jesus—eventually he not only heard, he believed!

It may be difficult, but I have good reason to see hope for these couples. I have seen God create spiritual harmony in seemingly impossible circumstances. We are privileged to encourage these couples to accept and respect their differences. At the same time, we can encourage them both to seek God in the way He wants to be found.

The living Lord promises to reveal Himself to those who seek Him with all their heart (Jeremiah 29:13). That is a promise worth sharing.

So welcome to the great adventure of ministry to Jewish-Gentile couples! (Sometimes referred to in the following pages as JGCs.) Expect plenty of ups and downs, but remember the story of Mark and Susan—and never doubt what God can do!

1.Vaughn R.A. Call and Tim B. Heaton, "Religious Influence on Marriage Stability," *Journal for the Scientific Study of Religion* 36:3 (1997): 390.

2. Enoch Wan and Tuvya Zaretsky, *Jewish-Gentile Couples: Trends, Challenges and Hopes* (Pasadena: William Carey Library Press 2004).

3. I realize that some who do not share this belief might pick this book up out of curiosity, possibly even as the Jewish "half" of a Jewish-Gentile couple. If that's you, I want to say, "Shalom—welcome!"

There aren't any secrets in here. No one is out to manipulate you, convert you or take away your Jewishness. In fact, I hope Christian readers will grow in respect for Jewish culture as a result of reading this. Hopefully, you might find something here that will help you to find spiritual harmony with your Gentile partner, too!

Chapter 1
Becoming a Translator

Ever traveled to a foreign land where you didn't know the language at all—not even the most common words? It can be frustrating to listen to the simplest sentence and realize, "Babies and dogs could understand this better than I do." That's culture shock.

Why is it so difficult for Jewish-Gentile couples to understand one another, especially concerning matters of faith? Simply this: they might seem to speak the same language, but they are coming from two very different cultures. Those cultures actually assign their own meanings—and sometimes emotional weight—to words. The result is, two people can listen to the same sentence and actually hear two different meanings.

We want to create understanding between ourselves and the Jewish-Gentile couples we minister to, while helping them do the same in their relationship with one another. That requires cross-cultural communication, something you can learn to do effectively if you don't yet know how. You'll discover how to bring clarity to conversations where meaning has become obscured by cultural differences. In other words, you'll become a cross-cultural translator.

Ministry to Jewish-Gentile couples might seem pretty straightforward; one partner is Jewish and the other isn't. But no, it gets complex. Some couples are simply dating and others live together. Couples with children face different challenges from those who don't. The couple's parents and other family members can also affect situations and circumstances. And just about the time you think it couldn't get any more complicated, don't be surprised when along comes a same-sex Jewish-Gentile couple. I've encountered all those situations and have ministered to people in each one.[1]

Getting Started

Let's begin with the premise that all communication is cross-cultural. Each person has a personal, cultural perspective of the world and how it should be. Each culture has its own sets of understanding. Realizing how that affects everyone's perspective is an important step to finding common ground.

You need to understand the cultural differences between Jewish-Gentile partners, and so do they. To illustrate the differences, I invite couples to participate in a little exercise. You might find it helpful to do the same.

I ask couples to choose a word that they already know they don't agree upon, and then take turns describing what that word means to them. The word doesn't need to have any spiritual connotation; in fact, if you're going to use this as an icebreaker, it probably helps if it doesn't.

Meet Hannah and Ted, who picked the word "dog."

Hannah was Jewish and from Beverly Hills. Her dog, Princess, lived up to her name. She ate off the family table and slept in Hannah's bed. Hannah spoke affectionately of her dog, describing her as a precious member of the family.

Two people can listen to the same sentence and actually hear two different meanings.

Ted wasn't Jewish, and came from a very different part of Los Angeles. He winced as Hannah described her pampered pet. Where Ted grew up, dogs had a very particular function. The name of his dog, Fang, was a good indicator of that function. Fang lived in the front yard and his job was to guard the house. He ate table scraps (i.e., garbage) from the floor. The idea of allowing the dog to sleep in a family member's bed was inconceivable.

Hannah and Ted cared for each other a lot. They could banter good-naturedly about Princess and Fang, but they also recognized how their different cultures and experiences provided two completely different sets of thoughts and feelings about dogs.

Discussions about how a dog fits into the family structure could be humorous—or intense. Just imagine the intensity of discussing key issues of identity and religious differences. Cross-cultural misunderstandings on those deeper matters can be painful.

Helping People Talk "to" Not "at" Each Other

One really earnest Christian guy told me—in the presence of his Jewish girlfriend—that he really loved her, so he didn't want her to go to hell. It was important to him that she "get saved." It frustrated him that, though they both were speaking English, she didn't understand what he was trying to tell her.

Now, his girlfriend is a very bright woman. She heard those words, but she had neither a cultural nor a theological basis to understand them. I explained to him that Judaism doesn't focus much on heaven or hell, or salvation as Christians understand it. This came as news to him. He also presumed that she shared his appreciation for the Bible. She didn't!

That couple perfectly illustrated the religious differences that couples identified as one of their top five challenges.

More than 30 years ago, Rabbi Shamai Kanter of Congregation Beth El in Rochester, New York, wrote, "The subject of God and personal belief is effectively taboo, as much prohibited from polite conversation as once were death, sex or cancer."[2]

This is still very true for many Jewish people, who often prefer not to talk about God, the Bible, or the hereafter. When Jewish people hear others discuss these things, the most common response is, "That's fine if it makes you happy," the implication being, "Please don't try to force your ideas on me." And the merest suggestion that those ideas are anything more than a preference or a personal perspective is easily perceived as forcing them on others.

While a Jewish partner might not practice the Jewish religion, the thought of embracing "someone else's" religion threatens the very core of his or her identity, which is another key challenge that Jewish-Gentile couples described.

Yet Christians, if they have genuine faith, see the Bible as God's revelation of what He wants for and from all people, regardless of culture and ethnicity. The hereafter is a source of great hope for all who have faith in Christ; therefore, love requires Christians to share that hope. Contemplating a loved one spending eternity apart from God is terribly painful. So the Christian's very identity, not only as a Christian, but as a loving partner, is also at stake. Each partner often unintentionally poses a perceived threat to the other's identity.

Each partner often unintentionally poses a perceived threat to the other's identity.

One might assume that all these things would be discussed early in the relationship. Yet one or both partners often set aside beliefs or priorities in order to enter into the very relationship where later, any revival of their beliefs and priorities may become a source of conflict.

What about the earnest Christian partner who kept telling his Jewish girlfriend that he wanted her to be saved so she wouldn't go to hell? He may as well have been speaking to her in a foreign language. Repeating his words with so much intensity and passion—and a degree of impatience—only made it worse for them both.

He didn't realize he was "pitching an idea" to (or at) someone who didn't have the capacity to grasp it. Of course he never meant to be unkind. When he realized what he'd been doing, he shook his head saying, "I was just pretty 'Jewish stupid.'" Actually, like his girlfriend, he's pretty bright—but their attempts to understand one another were frustrated by assumptions and use of Christian jargon.

Meanwhile, his Jewish partner was trapped in her own cultural presumptions. She saw his attempts to "convert her" as brutish and ignorant. She felt he was intolerant of her Jewish culture. All she could say in response was, "He is just so goyish!" That is, "He is just so . . . Gentile (who doesn't understand Jews)." She had no interest in exploring his worldview.

So how can we serve Jewish-Gentile partners in this situation?

Creating Clarity

Crossword puzzles entertain us with clever double meanings. A clue such as "a four-letter word for a big horn" teases an answer of either "bull" or "tuba." We, on the other hand, want to do the opposite: find a precise meaning for words, one that creates understanding.

So how do we begin?

Beware of using insider language to describe people as "unbelievers" or "unsaved." Help the couples avoid jargon as well. Because frankly, even jargon-free conversations still leave more than enough room for misunderstanding or talking past one another. Remember the concept of foreign languages in cross-cultural communication.

I've told small groups of JGCs, "We are in a safe environment; we can ask questions here without being judged. If someone in the group, including your spouse or me, uses a term that you don't understand, just say so. We'll stop and find out what it means." You'll want to create that atmosphere/opportunity for the couples you meet.

Beware of using insider language to describe people as "unbelievers" or "unsaved."

You don't always have to wait for people to ask what a word means. If someone uses the word *Christ* I'll ask, "What do you understand the word *Christ* to mean?" The Gentile/sometimes-Christian partner often says something like, "*Christ* means 'Savior,' doesn't it?" A Jewish partner often sheepishly responds, "That's something I say when I'm frustrated."

By the way, the response of the Jewish partner above was very much my own experience for many years. And before I was old enough to think of His name as an expletive? Forgive me, but as a little kid, I thought Christ was Jesus' last name.

Anyway, after each couple responds to the question, I can then explain that the word *Christ* is an English word with several dictionary meanings. It can refer to a painting of "the *Christ*," or, as mentioned by the Jewish partner, it can refer to an expletive. But the original meaning—the one that's relevant to our conversation—comes from the Greek word *Christos*, which means "Anointed One." And in fact, that is exactly what *Messiah* means. In other words, *Christos* was the Greek term that Bible translators used for the Hebrew word *Mashiach*.

Bottom line, *Christ* was originally a Jewish concept.

Something as simple as a mutual understanding of the word *Christ* can give a couple confidence that, together, they can find meaningful and common terms with which to discuss spiritual truth. That opens up a door for hope.

Similarly, you can ask each partner, "When you say *Christian*, how do you define or understand that word?" I've actually heard both Jewish and Gentile partners say, "A Christian is someone who believes in Christ." Don't leave it at that; it's vague and can still mean something entirely different to each partner. Clarify the question by asking what "believes in Christ" means to each. A Jewish person might think it's just something that Gentiles do. And some Gentiles might think it is something that "religious people do," without knowing the theological content of such belief.

After listening carefully, repeat what you've heard each partner say. Then, without correcting anyone, offer your own definition. Don't rely on your cultural understanding but where appropriate, refer to sources such as dictionaries, Bible dictionaries, theological wordbooks, encyclopedias and Bibles.

The aim is to arrive at a mutual definition of key words, one that is not based on either person's cultural perceptions. We are seeking to create clarity, first in our terminology and then later about concepts and spiritual ideas.

Again, the steps are,

- Ask each partner for their definition or understanding of a key term
- Listen without interrupting
- Repeat what you heard without correcting
- Offer your own understanding of the word, bringing in an outside source to show an objective definition
- Ask for agreement on a mutual understanding of the word

You can adapt those same steps to create clarity, not just around words, but also around concerns that seem obvious to one partner but foreign to the other.

I ask each partner to check the communication processes by stating a spiritual concern, and then asking the other person, "How do you understand what I'm telling you?" It isn't a matter of parroting words back to prove they were listening. It's finding out what those words meant to the other person. I let both partners know, "If what you hear back is not the meaning you intended, don't repeat the same words. It'll only frustrate both of you. And whatever you do, don't keep repeating the same words, only louder!" I've actually seen that happen!

A third party can help bring clarity as well as compassion into the conversation. For example:

Gentile Partner: "He's not really Jewish. He doesn't even believe in God."
Me: "Wow. Do you have any idea how that sounds to him? And why do you say that?"
Gentile Partner: "Well, he doesn't even go to his church."
Me: "Do you mean he never goes to his synagogue?"

Gentile Partner: "Right. He doesn't go to his synagogue. Sorry about that."
Me: (*to the Jewish partner*) "How do you respond to what she said?"
Jewish Partner: "It's pretty harsh. It's not like I never go to synagogue. I go on the High Holy Days . . . sometimes. My relationship with God just isn't like hers. I pray, but I don't talk to God like she does."
Me: (*to the Gentile*) "So, what do you think about what he's telling you?"
Gentile Partner: "I'm sorry for judging you. It's just that I don't get how you are Jewish or what religion means for you."
Me: "That's a good direction for this conversation to go. We can talk about what makes someone Jewish. We can also try for better understanding of what religion means for each of your identities."

Again, there's that word: *identities*. It's a core concern.

Dispelling Stereotypes

Everyone comes to a relationship with ideas about the other person's cultural identity. When those ideas are formed without actually interacting with the other culture, they tend to be stereotypes. Stereotypes can be either positive or negative. They create a quick, general understanding (or misunderstanding) of someone from a foreign culture. When one partner doesn't match up with the expected stereotype, it produces discomfort and confusion for both partners.

Gentiles often expect Jews to be somehow defined by or connected to the religion of Judaism even when the attachment is thinner than a microchip. Jewish partners tend to assume Gentiles are Christians (unless they declare themselves otherwise), and also that Christians are automatically Gentiles . . . even without knowing exactly what a Christian believes. If a Jewish partner's attachment to his or her religion is nominal, it's easy to assume that the Gentile partner's religion is likewise a "given" of cultural identity, and not necessarily deeply held conviction.

In any case, neither is likely to understand the key words or concepts used to describe their partner's identity.

That's why introductory conversations about terminology are so important, and why you'll want to go through the process outlined above to help Jewish-Gentile couples understand one another's key words and concepts.

I have some advantage in seeing how people talk past each other because Christianity was once very foreign to me. If a person expressed concern for me to get saved, I might have silently wondered, "Saved from what?" but more likely I'd have dismissed it as something un-Jewish and therefore irrelevant to me. To them, there was a theological issue at stake; to me, avoiding any invitation to consider their beliefs was necessary to my cultural identity and survival as a Jew.

Always remember that everyone has acquired a set of understandings or beliefs about where they came from, the meanings of words, the right way to do things and what beliefs and practices are proper and appropriate to maintain their identity. That acquired set of understandings is known as *enculturation*.

The differences between two partners' enculturation hugely impacts their relationship. It's the reason one partner can be shocked and confused by the other's reaction to words that seem harmless or even positive. The greater the differences in culture, the greater the communication gap and potential misunderstanding. The challenge for each partner is to see the other from a new perspective, a different one than they have assumed based on their own culture.

We who hope to minister among JGCs have our own expectations about what their religious conviction "ought to be." That "ought-ness" is a result of our own cultural training, so remember that words and ideas that may seem obvious to us will not be understood the same way by one or both partners.

You need to understand the cultural differences between Jewish-Gentile partners, and so do they.

We want to present truth in ways that people can hear from their own cultural context. As you serve Jewish-Gentile couples, you are going to grapple with three cultures: the Jewish partner's, the Gentile partner's and your own culture. In order to do that, you have to be aware of your own culture. Because until we know our own culture, we aren't able to appreciate other cultures.

Imagine someone whose culture is to drink coffee every morning. He normally refers to it as "my cuppa." He stays at a friend's house overnight and in the morning says, "Can I trouble you for a cuppa?" The friend says "sure" and brews him a cup of strong tea. The guy looks at it a bit suspiciously but takes a sip. Spitting it out, he exclaims, "That's the worst coffee I've ever tasted!"

Get it? The guy didn't realize that drinking coffee was his culture; he assumed that it was the only "cuppa" out there. So he couldn't recognize—much less appreciate—tea. To him, it was just lousy coffee. We don't want to be that guy! Nor would we want to be a guy who knows what coffee is, and knows his friend prefers it, but thinks it's boorish to drink anything but tea in the morning. That would be ethnocentric.

Anthropologists describe *ethnocentrism* as the perspective that one's own culture is civilized and others are primitive or backward. Paul Hiebert said, "This response has to do with attitudes, not with understandings."[3] As with many attitudes, those who are ethnocentric usually don't know it; their culture includes unexamined assumptions.

Don't mistake me: I'm not saying that all cultures have different but equally true ideas about how to know God. How to get caffeine and how to know God are very different things! I'm just saying that if we are unaware of our own culture, we're setting ourselves up to misunderstand other people who have a different culture, because we'll assume they share our definitions and ideas.

Conclusion

You're on your way to becoming a good cross-cultural translator as you begin to identify what important issues Jewish-Gentile partners see differently because of their cultures.

Whether you have a lot or a little to learn, I hope you are excited to become a cross-cultural translator and a communication bridge-builder. You don't have to know everything about other people's cultures to do this effectively, as long as you remember to:

- avoid assumptions about shared understanding of words, even common ones (especially religious jargon). Instead,
- create understanding by taking turns explaining what key words mean (or don't mean) to each person.
- Avoid assumptions about shared ideas and concerns. Instead,
- create clarity by asking one partner to state a spiritual concern, then asking the other what they understand their partner to be saying.

Remember too that as believers, we are relying on the Spirit of God to communicate His truth. Sometimes, He even does that through us!

Exercise

For this and subsequent exercises, use a separate sheet of paper where necessary. (Many chapters have ample blank space on the last page.) Answer the following questions to help you see what your own background and experience brings to the cross-cultural communications table.

Part A

How would you describe your own ethnicity?

Did you grow up in a Christian home?

How long have you been a Christian?

Did you have misconceptions about Christians or Christianity before you received Christ? If so, what were they?

Did you grow up with any particular religious traditions? If so, describe them and their importance to you as a child. Are they still part of your life today? Why or why not?

If you are Gentile, do you have any relatives, close friends or colleagues who are Jewish? If not, do you have any basic impressions of Jewish people/culture and if so, what is the basis for those impressions?

If you are Jewish, do you have any relatives, close friends or colleagues who are Gentile? What is your basis for impressions concerning non-Jewish people/culture?

Have you ever been in a situation where you felt a central aspect of your identity was challenged or threatened? If yes, recall the circumstance and what that was like.

Now list ten facts about yourself apart from your ethnic or spiritual identity. Include where you were raised, schools attended, profession, hobbies, travel you've done, etc.

Part B

Think about a Jewish-Gentile couple you hope to reach. Use the diagram on the next page. Fill in the Jewish partners' name in the top left quadrant of the page and the Gentile partner's name in the top right quadrant. In light of your answers to the above questions, use those two top quadrants to list the possible ways your own culture and experience might help you understand each partner.

Use the bottom two quadrants to list ways that you might respond to your lack of knowledge about one or both partners' culture(s). (For example, "ask questions that will help me understand _______'s perspective on what it means to him/her to attend church/synagogue.)

---

1. Ministry to people in situations that we do not condone is a huge challenge. If you find yourself in need of feedback regarding a particularly difficult situation, speak to your pastor or feel free to contact me and I'll help if I can. Bottom line: you'll have to decide which, if any, situations you feel would best be handled by someone else.
2. Shamai Kanter, "They're Playing Our Song," *Moment* 3/84:30.
3. Paul G. Hiebert, *Anthropological Insights for Missionaries* (Grand Rapids: Baker Book House, 1985), 97–99.

Jewish partner's name: ______________________	Gentile partner's name: ______________________

Chapter 2
Basic Vocabulary

You've seen that in cross-cultural communication, basic vocabulary is anything but basic. You are now ready to enter into the discussion as an equal partner and discover what key words mean to all three of you, in each of your cultures. You are ready to create mutual understanding around those words.

This chapter focuses on a collection of important words and phrases, what they mean, and how they can be understood or misunderstood.

For example, it's not uncommon for a Jewish partner to say, "I could never become a Christian." The Gentile partner might hear this as, "I could never become like you." You, the cross-cultural translator, might think it means, "I could never follow Jesus." But the Jewish person might mean—and probably does mean—something very different.

I grew up hearing my parents used the word "Christian" as a synonym for Gentile (non Jew). That was and still is a pretty typical Jewish outlook. A Jewish person who says, "I could never become a Christian" might actually mean, "I will never stop being a Jew." Which, by the way, is not the same as, "I will never stop following the Jewish religion." Why? Because being Jewish has to do with ethnicity and is not determined by religion. Many Jewish people consider Judaism to be "my religion" mainly inasmuch as that is what they would practice if they wanted to become religious.

Understanding Ethnicity and Culture

Sorting out the differences between ethnicity and culture can help couples grow in their understanding of one another. Think of ethnicity in terms of a specific brand of computer hardware (such as IBM or Apple). Culture is like the software that enables a computer to process data. Culture empowers people to function in life. However, aspects of culture can be "updated" in order to process new data.

As people see their identity in these terms, it can diminish fears about losing their individual identities in the quest for shared understanding.

Following are some terms I've defined to help you get the most from this workbook, along with comments on how they relate to the couples you want to minister to. I'm including words that we began discussing in chapter 1. Understanding these key words will expand your cross-cultural knowledge and help you make discoveries about your own culture.

Key Words

Ethnicity

Ethnicity is the nationality of a people or an individual in that group. Bloodline is the determining factor.

When it comes to ethnicity, being Jewish is based on DNA and Jewish ancestry. It is possible for a non-Jew to convert to the Jewish religion, and even to take on aspects of Jewish culture, but ethnicity is a matter of birth.

Intermarriage introduces variations in bloodlines and cultural changes. Over time, intermarriage and assimilation have led to the gradual disappearance of some ethnic groups from history. For example, how many Hittites do you know? Nevertheless, despite intermarriage the Jewish people have survived.

Culture

Culture is the accumulation of acquired behaviors, social structures, personal experiences and core beliefs.

Cultural patterns are shared ideas and behaviors about the way things ought to be. They begin developing before we even realize that we are absorbing cultural "facts." Parents are forming a child's culture when they show how to hold a fork or model a language or dialect. It was culture that moved Goldilocks (from the story of "Goldilocks and the Three Bears") to prefer Baby Bear's porridge as not too hot and not too cold, but "just right." Culture lets people know the "just rightness" of their artifacts, behaviors and beliefs.

Ethnicity and culture are often mistakenly used interchangeably. While the two are often related, they are not the same thing.

All culture is learned. It lets us know what is appropriate, be it behavior or fashion. It forms our attitudes about important subjects, including how we describe ourselves. It shapes the understandings of our origin and the cosmos. Every human being collects their particular culture over a lifetime, making those components unique to every person.

Ethnicity and *culture* are often mistakenly used interchangeably. While the two are often related, they are not the same thing.

A good test of whether something is ethnicity or culture is to ask if people can change it. In the case of beliefs, including religious beliefs, people can and do change them. Since religion is held at the deepest level or core of a culture, such change is counter to social expectations and carries consequences. That's why any suggestion of change can be perceived as a threat. Still, people's religion can change, because culture can and does change and religion is a cultural component.

Religion

Religion is a system of beliefs and worship. Since science hasn't identified a religion gene, neither bloodline nor DNA will determine from birth what people must believe or how they will express those beliefs. A particular religion may be strongly associated with a particular ethnic group, but religion is still an aspect of culture, not ethnicity.

Religion is a system of beliefs and worship.

For example, my wife Ellen and I are both Ashkenazi, that is, descended from East European Jews. Ellen's obstetrician warned her that she was a potential carrier of a specific genetic mutation that could have adversely affected our children. He wanted her tested for the possible specific Jewish genetic defect. Her OB was Jewish, and may have found Ellen's Messianic (Jewish Christian) religious beliefs culturally confusing. But his advice regarding genetic testing was based on his understanding that Ellen's ethnicity was established by her Jewish genes, not through her religious beliefs.

Jew

In the context of this book, the term *Jew* denotes a person of ethnic descent from Abraham, Isaac and Jacob. It is a designation based on bloodline. You should know, however, that the question, "Who is a Jew?" can be confusing, because in popular discussion it is often assigned religious, social, cultural and political distinctions.

Jewish religion

Jewish culture and Jewish religion are sometimes viewed as synonymous. Religion is a framework that helped preserve Jewish people while they were scattered in exile among other nations for more than two thousand years. Judaism (that is, the Jewish religion) is important to Jewish culture and tradition, and is closely identified with Jewish people. Again, the Jewish religion is not a criterion for determining Jewish ethnicity.

Judaism

The term *Judaism* as mentioned above is a designation for the Jewish religion. However, it is associated with a wide range of definitions, both religious and secular, and frankly the diversity of culture within the Jewish people prevents a simple, monolithic definition. In this workbook, we will try to use the term *Judaism* in its narrowest sense, as the traditional religion of many, but not all, Jewish people. It will be helpful for you to understand that it may have many other meanings to the Jewish side of the Jewish-Gentile couples you meet.

Jewish

This term is an adjective to describe distinctive features associated with Jews or Jewish people. It may relate to an ethnic matter, such as the Jewish gene already mentioned. More commonly, it refers to something cultural, like Jewish food or even Jewish humor.

Gentile
This term is taken from the Hebrew term *goy*, which means "nation" and is considered grammatically correct with a small *g*. (The plural of *goy* is *goyim*.) It could refer to any nation. However, when the Bible speaks of "the nations" it is typically speaking to Israel about the rest of the nations. The Jewish perspective of the word *Gentile* follows that distinction, so a Gentile is anyone who is not a Jew. In this workbook, it's spelled with a capital *G* to avoid any perceived inequality when speaking of Jews and Gentiles as people groups.

Gentiles do not ordinarily think of themselves as "Gentiles"; after all, identifying as a non-Jew would be a non-issue for most. Yet, from a Jewish perspective, there are two categories of people, simply Jews and Gentiles, though sometimes that is expressed as "us" and "them."

Christ
The term *Christ* has a powerful, biblical meaning. It speaks of the one who was anointed by God for a particular salvation purpose. As mentioned in chapter 1, it is the Greek translation of *Messiah*.

Against that backdrop, Jews and Gentiles can more easily comprehend the Jewish context of Yeshua (Jesus) as the Lord's anointed Redeemer, the Messiah.

Jesus
Similarly, the word *Yeshua,* "Jesus," has a meaning. Did you know that it literally means "Savior"? Most Jewish people don't know that. Nor do most know what a Savior does unless or until we have conversation about it.

How did Jesus get His name? Matthew 1:18–21 tells how an angel of the Lord announced the name "Savior" or *Yeshua* in Hebrew, to Him. Why did He need to come and save anybody? The same Bible passage reports that Jesus, or Yeshua, came to "save His people from their sins." That was the promise about the Servant Messiah 750 years earlier as reported in Isaiah 53:5–6.

Christian
A Christian is a follower of Jesus the Messiah, whose death and resurrection are the basis for forgiveness and a relationship with God. A Christian can be from any ethnic group. This is crucial; once someone understands the word *Christian* to mean one of the Messiah's followers, it becomes clear that not all Gentiles are Christians, and that both Jews and non-Jews (Gentiles) can be Christian or Messianic. That can open a window for a Jewish person to see a brand new picture of their Gentile partner, or you, as a Christian.

A Christian can be from any ethnic group.

Messianic
This adjective can be used to describe anything pertaining to "messiah" in general, but more often is used in relation to the Messiah, Yeshua (Jesus). *Messianic* often describes a type of congregation where traditional Jewish liturgies are used to worship Him. The word also describes

Jewish people who follow Jesus, or even Gentile Christians who identify strongly with the Jewish roots of their faith.

Interfaith

This term is used to describe couples, communities or events (such as dialogues) that represent more than one religion. Interfaith couples are not necessarily married nor are they necessarily different ethnicities.

Be aware that this term is often used incorrectly, as in "interfaith dialogue between Christians and Jews." That phrase creates a false dichotomy because it mixes a religious/cultural category (Christians) with one that is ethnic (Jews). It is a classic "apples to oranges" comparison. In fact, some Jews are Christians, as opposed to being one or the other.

A secular Jewish-Gentile couple is not accurately described as interfaith, since neither partner holds to a religious commitment. Nor would the term accurately apply to Jewish-Gentile partners who share the same religious faith. So then, a Messianic Jew and a Gentile Christian are not an interfaith couple. They actually share the same religion, though they are ethnically different.

A secular Jewish-Gentile couple is not accurately described as interfaith, since neither partner holds to a religious commitment.

Not everyone gets these distinctions, but once you understand them, you'll be able to bring clarity to conversations that utilize these terms.

Intermarriage

This term can describe any number of unions, but for the purpose of this workbook, it is a marriage between a Jewish and Gentile partner. In the Jewish community this is sometimes called "marrying out." Intermarriage doesn't have to refer to religious differences, but it often includes them.

However, from the traditional Jewish community perspective, the faith of Judaism is usually presumed on the Jewish partner (even if they are secular) and so an intermarriage would be presumed interfaith unless a Gentile partner had converted to Judaism.

With these definitions in mind, I have chosen the term *Jewish-Gentile couples* as the simplest, most consistent way to describe the broad range of people this workbook is designed help you reach.

Note: see appendix 1 for a more in-depth understanding of some of these terms.

Emotions Surrounding These Terms

We can unintentionally stir up emotion if we forget that couples can have very different understandings of key words, or if we don't realize how some of these words speak to core issues of identity. Navigating these meanings is part of the cross-cultural adventure.

Sensitivity to the terminology that Jewish-Gentile couples use to describe themselves is one of the first things you need to know about working with them. But even when you are sensitive and knowledgeable, don't be surprised if some anger flares up. It might be part of an ongoing reaction to previous conversations and situations between the couple.

When a partner becomes angry, it's a signal to speak softly and try to understand what that person heard. The anger might be a signal that the conversation is hitting a real issue that is close to that partner's core values. If a Jewish person grew up believing, as I did, "You can't be Jewish and believe in Jesus," then suggesting that Jesus is for Jews hits the Jewish core value of survival. You probably want to go very slow in the conversation at that point. You are treading on very sensitive ground! But don't stop, either!

Sometimes anger is used, intentionally or not, to derail a conversation that is perceived as a threat. You can ask questions in order to understand what the partner is hearing. Then ask for their permission to continue the discussion with sensitivity. You might be able to diffuse the perceived threat. But you should also be prepared to defer the discussion to a later time when it is less likely to be volatile. (For more about how to understand and respond to angry reactions, see appendix 5 on stumbling blocks and challenges.)

Sometimes anger is used, intentionally or not, to derail a conversation that is perceived as a threat.

Anger is sometimes a reaction to pain. One partner might not even realize that she or he has caused pain, and therefore does not understand the anger. Other times one partner will become negative because the other has unintentionally insulted or offended.

For example I heard one Christian partner refer to her Jewish spouse as an "unbeliever." He was sitting right next to her and was righteously offended!

From the Christian's perspective, that description was apt. But can you imagine how it sounded to the Jewish guy? He took his wife's reference as judgmental and incredibly hurtful. The husband couldn't hear past the insult to ever get to the gospel.

Avoiding Clichés

We need to help JGCs find and use words that enable them to understand what their partners mean to say. That includes helping them avoid clichés or jargon that can act like improvised explosive devices (IEDs).

Clichés are generally overused expressions that have little meaning to people outside the particular culture that uses them. For example, the phrase "My Lord and Savior, Jesus Christ" doesn't connect with a Jewish person. They may have heard the words before, but that doesn't mean they have a basis to know what they mean, other than they are Christian expressions, or part of Christian culture. As such, the words lose their impact. To the Christian, those terms are shorthand for a meaningful personal relationship. The shorthand just doesn't convey to others the wonder of trusting a loving God.

We can look beyond the usual culture-laden terminology by carefully choosing beautiful, significant and meaningful terms that are not necessarily part of either culture. This builds bridges to understanding.

Conclusion

Becoming acquainted with the words in this chapter will help in your role as cross-cultural translator, as you put into practice the principles you learned in chapter 1. The distinction between ethnicity and culture is one that you'll need to help couples remember again and again. Cultural biases and stereotypes do not disappear overnight, but your patience will make a difference as couples learn to listen to and question one another with the intent to understand.
Remember also that choosing our words for what they mean, rather than using easy clichés, is a great place to begin to create understanding.

Exercise

The terms *salvation* and *being saved* mean very little to the average Jewish person and may not have much meaning or appeal to the average Gentile either.

In what ways do you experience God's salvation daily? Make a list of words to describe as many aspects of personal salvation as you can. Based on that list, and on truth that you know from Scripture, choose words that are beautiful, significant and meaningful to write several sentences that describe what being saved means to you. Don't use the words *salvation* or *being saved*.

Take the most important and compelling parts of what you have written and compress them into just one or two sentences.

Using a Bible dictionary and concordance, do your own study on the meaning of salvation in the Bible so that you can explain the Hebrew concept of salvation and have a few key verses to point to. You can also go online: http://www.godandscience.org/doctrine/salvat.html.

Pray for opportunities to share your personal experience as well as what the Bible says about salvation or being saved. Be prepared, because it's likely that a JGC will mention the word or phrase, either as a concern or as a point of confusion between them. Remember that your role as a cross-cultural translator means helping each partner hear what the other is trying to say, as well as sharing your own ideas of the word, then offering an objective definition.

---

1. Jim Aylesworth, *Goldilocks and the Three Bears* (New York: Scholastic Press, 2003.), 1.

Chapter 3
Biblical Concepts, a Cross-Cultural Comparison

Besides a working understanding of key words, you'll also need a collection of biblical concepts, which will surface when the conversation turns to matters touching on religious differences and/or the possibility of spiritual harmony. Like "basic vocabulary," these concepts might seem obvious to you—but might mean something very different to each partner.

Take the idea of prayer, for example. You know what prayer looks like. And if the Gentile partner is a Christian they, too, know what prayer looks like. Heads are bowed and eyes are closed. Words flow from the heart of the believer straight to God. But when partners come from two different cultures, what they are accustomed to hearing and saying in prayer (if they were raised with prayer of any kind) will be very different. Even Christians tend to pick up phrases and ways of speaking to God that are comfortable and meaningful to them but may sound a bit strange in the ears of another Christian.

Imagine how different the concept of prayer is for someone who does not come from a Christian culture at all.

If the Jewish partner learned to pray in a traditional manner they are most comfortable with everyone reading from a *siddur* (prayer book), with all eyes open.

Introducing a Bible text into a discussion with Jewish-Gentle couples brings the fourth culture to the conversation, on top of the cultures familiar to each partner and to you. God communicated His intent through the minds, personalities and writing instruments of human beings. In order to understand and communicate what God intended in the text, we have to keep that in mind, along with an awareness of the cultural understandings of each partner.

When presenting a scriptural account of a key concept, you will find yourself serving as a cross-cultural translator once again. Listen to what each person understands or believes about the concept, translate between them and then let them hear what the text has to say. I prefer to let the text speak for itself. For more on this subject see, "Let the Text Speak for Itself" at http://www.gospel-life.net/let-the-text-speak-for-itself/.

The following list of Bible topics for discussion is a starting place to show the cross-cultural aspect of discussing biblical truths with JGCs. I hope it will encourage you to become more familiar with Jewish cultural perspectives while examining Bible passages and spiritual concepts.

Conversion

Most Jewish people would never dream of "converting" because it conveys the idea of turning away from our Jewish people to join a foreign religion. It implies rejection of the Jewish people along with the God of Israel in favor of a non-Jewish culture and the god of those who embrace that religion. It is seen as social abandonment of Jewish family and community. Traitors convert.

That said, you won't be surprised when a Jewish person says to you, "I would never convert." But how can you respond? Try asking them, "What does the word *convert* mean to you?" Then listen carefully to what they tell you about their understanding. Affirm what you can. Even though you may have an idea of what they are going to say, it's important that they be able to express what they mean, and that their partner hears it. The partner should also have an opportunity to say what she or he thinks about the idea of conversion.

When partners come from two different cultures, what they are accustomed to hearing and saying in prayer will be very different.

You might mention that the modern Hebrew terms for conversion are *b'tshuva shivah* (Bee-chew-vah, she-vah), literally "repent and return." That raises an interesting question: what is the point of departure and to what does one return?

If they are open to what the Bible says, show them a passage or two that illustrates the original meaning. Try to avoid saying anything that would seem to negate their prior understanding or feelings about conversion. Ask if perhaps these Scriptures have opened up a different understanding of the concept. Most are unaware that the biblical concept of conversion is to "repent and return." That is, "repent of your sin and return to the Lord."[1]

Ezekiel 14:6 is a good example of the command to turn from transgression: "Therefore say to the house of Israel, 'Thus says the Lord God: "Repent, turn away from your idols, and turn your faces away from all your abominations."' You'd also find it in Ezekiel 18:30: "'Therefore I will judge you, O house of Israel, every one according to his ways,' says the Lord God. 'Repent and turn from all your transgressions, so that iniquity will not be your ruin.'"

That same Biblical idea appears in the New Testament, where Simon Peter speaks to a crowd of Jewish people in Jerusalem on the Day of Pentecost. He explains the good news of Messiah Jesus to the Israelites in Acts 3:19–20 saying, "Repent therefore and be converted, that your sins may be blotted out, so that times of refreshing may come from the presence of the Lord, and that He may send Jesus Christ, who was preached to you before."

King David wrote with great personal transparency about turning from sin to God in Psalm 51:1–13. This very personal confession by Israel's greatest king recounts his sin of coveting another man's wife, having an adulterous affair with her and then murdering her husband.

King David describes what it was like to repent of his sin and ask for God's forgiveness and a restored intimacy with Him. David's admission of guilt is passionate and heartfelt. His longing for forgiveness and spiritual renewal are powerful. It's a conversion experience. We know that because David promises that when God restores the joy of his salvation, he (David) will teach other sinners how to be converted. "Then I will teach transgressors Your ways, and sinners shall be converted to You" (Psalm 51:13).

In the Bible, conversion has nothing to do with turning away from being a Jew, and everything to do with turning away from sin. That brings us to another key concept where you'll see very different interpretations.

Most are unaware that the biblical concept of conversion is to "repent and return."

Sin

Would it surprise you to know that many Jewish people (and non-Jewish people as well) do not consider themselves sinners? It isn't that they have a lofty opinion of themselves, it's that they have no theological basis for understanding what sin is. If you were to ask, "What do you think sin is?" it's likely that they would recite criminal behaviors, such as stealing or murder. Few would be able to tell you a biblical understanding of sin ("missing the mark"). Fewer still would be able to relate to "the mark" as a standard defined by God and His righteousness.

Traditional Judaism teaches a sort of moral dualism in which two natures are at work within every human being. One is the evil inclination and the other is the good inclination (Yetzir HaRa and Yetzir HaTov). Everyone is free to choose between those natures and is charged with the responsibility of choosing to do good. So traditional Jewish views portray sin as the product of human choices.

Sin is often seen as the opposite of good deeds. Along with that is the perception that some sins are not really significant, as they do not harm others. It is interesting that people expect God to be concerned about the sin that we obviously commit against other people without realizing that every sin we commit is a sin against God. It is His standards that we are violating if we mistreat one another or even if we mistreat ourselves.

One of the easiest ways to understand sin is simply this: anything we think, do or say that undermines what God wants for us or from us. That includes disinterest in knowing Him, feeling that He has no business setting standards of right and wrong, etc. In other words, sin is everywhere. Sin against God is at the root of every wicked and hurtful thing that people do to one another.

The Bible reveals that the human heart is broken and selfish, in rebellion against God. It describes human nature as broken or dysfunctional to its very core. Our thoughts, words and actions are influenced by that corrupt and broken nature. This does not mean that everything we do is wicked, but it does mean that evil comes naturally to us because of our broken condition.

The Bible reveals that the human heart is broken and selfish, in rebellion against God.

King David goes on record in Psalm 51:5: "Behold, I was brought forth in iniquity, and in sin my mother conceived me." King David isn't lamenting some imaginary bad deeds he committed the day he was born; he is recognizing his innate human nature and tendencies. When it comes to sin, many Jewish people believe that Judaism is superior to Christianity because Judaism appeals to a person's better nature while Christianity, it is thought, takes a low view of humanity. But the Christian view of sin and human nature is rooted in the Hebrew Scriptures.

What does the Bible say about the solution to sin?

Many people believe they can atone for sin or pay down the debt (what we owe by way of righteousness we lack) by doing good deeds. In contrast, the Bible says that none of us have enough in our spiritual bank account to clear up that deficit. Jesus said,

> For I say to you, that unless your righteousness exceeds the righteousness of the scribes and Pharisees, you will by no means enter the kingdom of heaven.
>
> You have heard that it was said to those of old, "You shall not commit murder and whoever murders will be in danger of the judgment." But I say to you that whoever is angry with his brother without a cause shall be in danger of the judgment. And whoever says to his brother, "Raca [empty head]!" shall be in danger of the council! But whoever says, "You fool!" shall be in danger of hell fire. (Matthew 5:20–22)

In other words, none of us are righteous enough on our own, and all of us face the consequences of our sin unless we receive God's gracious solution.[2]

Salvation

If someone does not understand what sin is or what it does, they certainly won't be able to see the need for salvation. Sin is our willful pulling away from God because we don't trust Him; it leaves us with a gaping wound instead of the connection to God we were meant to enjoy. Without that connection, we can never be whole. We are left without the presence of God in our lives; we are left without His peace and purpose. Salvation means we are delivered from the distress and spiritual death sin causes, brought back to spiritual life, and given full access to the presence, the peace and the purpose of God, in this life and in the next.

The Gospel

Jewish people typically think of this term as Christian jargon or in-speak. Many will refer to it as the "Christian gospel." From a Jewish perspective that implies the gospel is not for Jewish people, which undermines even the slightest interest to pursue or understand it. I hear plenty of Jewish people say, "Well, if I believe your gospel I won't be Jewish anymore." That's pretty much a nonstarter.

So, what would you want Jewish people to know about the term *gospel* that might create a new understanding? When capitalized, *Gospel* refers to one of the first four books in the New Testament, which are firsthand accounts of Jesus' life and ministry.

Here is something that may come as a surprise. *Gospel* is originally derived from the Hebrew term *besorah*, which literally means "good news." The Hebrew word was translated into the Greek Septuagint Bible as *euangelion*, for "good news." In the Latin Vulgate it was *evangelium*. Sometime before the twelfth century it came into the English language as *godspel*.

Here are a couple of terrific examples from the Hebrew Bible:

> O Zion,
> You who bring good tidings,
> Get up into the high mountain;
> O Jerusalem,
> You who bring good tidings,
> Lift up your voice with strength,
> Lift it up, be not afraid;
> Say to the cities of Judah, "Behold your God!" (Isaiah 40:9)

When the prophet Isaiah spoke about good news or the gospel in Bible texts, he was talking about the kingdom of God, His Messiah and salvation. In fact, Isaiah described the ministry of Messiah 750 years before Jesus came to earth. Among Isaiah's pointed descriptions of the Messianic mission, he wrote,

> The Spirit of the Lord GOD is upon Me,
> Because the LORD has anointed Me
> To preach good tidings to the poor;
> He has sent Me to heal the brokenhearted,
> To proclaim liberty to the captives.
> And the opening of the prison to those who are bound. (Isaiah 61:1)

Jesus was handed the book of Isaiah when visiting His home synagogue in Nazareth. He found the passage above, read it aloud and announced, "Today this Scripture is fulfilled in your hearing" (see Luke 4:16–21).

Eternal Life

In modern Jewish life and contemporary traditions of Judaism, eternal life is not an issue. The emphasis is on moral living here and now. *Tikkun Olam*, or "repairing the world" is an important Jewish doctrine. The implication is that God's creation is not perfect and that it is up to humanity to complete the job. Jewish people commonly ask, "What can I do to leave the world a better place than when I came into it?" Philanthropy and good deeds become essential to meaningful life now. Many Jewish people perceive Christianity as being unconcerned about these things, and unduly focused on heaven and hell.

Many Jewish people perceive Christianity as being unduly focused on heaven and hell.

That doesn't mean traditional Judaism has nothing to say about an afterlife. Commentaries do speak of "the World to Come"; however the idea is so far from being central to Judaism that for many, it's almost nonexistent. Loved ones live on in our memories and whatever legacy of good deeds they left on earth. The idea that people live on in any more concrete way might exist for some as an uncertain and vague hope.

Jesus, however, gave a very specific definition of eternal life: "And this is eternal life, that they may know You, the only true God, and Jesus Christ whom You have sent" (John 17:3). This idea did not come out of the blue, or from a non-Jewish source.

In the Torah, life as it is meant to be experienced comes through relationship with God. To know the Lord is to know life. To turn away from Him is to experience death and in particular, spiritual death. So God, through Moses, called the Israelites to "choose life" with Him.

> I call heaven and earth as witness today against you, that I have set before you life and death, blessing and cursing; therefore choose life that both you and your descendants may live, that you may love the LORD your God, that you may obey His voice, and that you may cling to Him, for He is your life and the length of your days; and that you may dwell in the land which the LORD swore to your fathers, to Abraham, Isaac, and Jacob, to give them. (Deuteronomy 30:19–20)

Jesus takes this concept of life and says we can experience it eternally. The Hebrew Scriptures hint here and there that there is hope for us to continue our relationship with God past our limited mortal lives (Job 19:25–26, Psalm 16:10).

God Is Good

Many people find it hard to understand how a good and gracious God could create a world that is infected with evil and death. They question how a good and all-powerful God could allow so much injustice, so much suffering in the world. I frequently hear Jewish people say, "I believe in God, but I just don't trust Him."

This topic is relevant in ministry to all kinds of people; if you aren't comfortable in responding, it's definitely worth taking time to do some outside reading. Many good books have been written on the subject. One of my favorites is *The Problem of Pain* by C. S. Lewis.

My own simple answer begins with a thought: God is purely good and nothing takes away from His goodness. We hear a phrase repeated in the Hebrew Bible giving praise to God in all circumstances, "Give thanks to the LORD, for He is good! For His mercy endures forever." God is sovereign and He is always good. (See Psalm 107:1 and Psalm 118.)

In fact, God is so good, loving and trustworthy that when He created human beings, He gave them a genuine free will. A fully intact free will that could be, and in fact, was wielded to ignore and disobey God. The consequence is brokenness. We are broken creatures who have willfully wrenched ourselves away from God. That is the root of brokenness in all human relationships. Our brokenness has infected our whole environment. God does not always intervene to prevent the kinds of things that naturally occur in a world that is in rebellion toward Him.

Messiah as Mediator

Rabbis often object to the role of Jesus as mediator and Son of God. The thinking goes, "We don't need an intermediary; we can go straight to God." Jesus would just be an irrelevant "middleman." This view does not take into account Moses, who interceded between God and Israel time after time. It doesn't acknowledge the validity of the entire priestly system found throughout the Hebrew Scriptures. Many have not read the Scriptures enough to know that such mediators were central to Jewish life and worship in Bible times. Those who do know might say that Judaism has evolved past the need for such things.

Our need for a mediator has to do with our broken fellowship with God, who does not change with our evolving ideas or perceptions.

Our need for a mediator has to do with our broken fellowship with God, who does not change with our evolving ideas or perceptions. This goes back to the concept of sin, and to the reality that the damage our sin causes can be healed only by God; we cannot heal or restore the relationship by our strength or according to our terms. If people are able to see that, the issue of a mediator is not a problem. The book of Hebrews gives detailed descriptions of Jesus interceding for us against the backdrop of Hebrew Scriptures.

The view that Judaism doesn't need a mediator is sometimes tossed out to derail the conversation—it's often a way of saying, "I'm not interested. What you believe about Jesus is irrelevant to me as a Jew." Before you take a great deal of time to explain why it is relevant, you'll want to check to be sure that there's some actual interest there.

God Is Immanent and Personal

"What do you want from God?" is a diagnostic question to discover what people believe about God. Ask the question of both partners and listen carefully to the answers. They will reveal whether the person believes that God is close and personally active in his or her life. Or they may reveal that they think of God as a mere concept, or a remote and indifferent cosmic being.

A big contrast between the partners' answers can account for some of the distance they might feel due to a lack of spiritual harmony. I often suggest that a partner who is open to discovering something new about God could pray, "God of Abraham, Isaac and Jacob, please show me who You are and what You want from me." It's pretty exciting when God chooses to answer that prayer. (More about this in chapter 6.)

Of course, the biblical view of God is of One who is both personal and immanent, who is near and close at hand. Walter C. Kaiser Jr. described God's relationship to Israel with a three-part formula. God repeats, "I will be your God, and you will be My people and I will dwell in the midst of you." Elements of this statement are repeated throughout the Scriptures from the Torah clear through to Revelation (Revelation 21:3).

> *We see in Isaiah 7:14 that the Messiah would also be known as "God with us," or Emmanuel.*

For some people, the idea that God wants to have this kind of relationship with them would be great news. Others prefer to think of God as distant and disinterested because it means they don't have to concern themselves with what God thinks, or what He might want for or from them.

Again, if people are willing to know what the Bible says about this, we see in Isaiah 7:14 that the Messiah would also be known as "God with us," or Immanuel. The Gospel of John says of Jesus, "The Word became flesh and dwelt among us, and we beheld His glory, the glory as of the only begotten of the Father, full of grace and truth" (John 1:14). The incarnate Messiah Jesus came to dwell in earth among humanity, and His *shekinah* glory was manifested. Jesus fulfilled Isaiah's Emmanuel promise.

The New Covenant

The new covenant is a glorious spiritual promise. While many Christians are familiar with the biblical idea of the new covenant, it is not normally discussed in traditional Jewish religious training. In a secular Jewish context, it is a foreign idea, if not totally unknown.

Whether or not the new covenant becomes a relevant topic depends on a person's interest in having any covenant with God. As with God's nearness and desire to be personally involved in our lives, it won't mean much to someone who is not yet interested in knowing God. But if someone is seeking, and is willing to consider what the Bible says about God's promises, it can be a good topic for discussion.

The prophet Jeremiah set the stage for this new covenant. He lived in the southern kingdom of Judah and entered into ministry for the Lord about 626 B.C. He witnessed the aftermath of Assyrian savagery against the Israelite northern kingdom of Samaria in 722 B.C. The Lord gave repeated warnings to the southern kingdom of Judah that it, too, would endure similar devastation and deportation if the people did not turn back to Yahweh.

These prophetic warnings sadly came to pass when the Babylonians invaded Judah in 586 B.C. Just as God had prophesied, the inhabitants of Judah saw Jerusalem sacked and the Temple destroyed along with the king's palace. In Jeremiah's thirty-first chapter, God promised to renew His covenant faithfulness with a remnant of Israel.

This covenant would be different from the Mosaic or Sinai covenant, which the inhabitants of Judah frequently broke. The new covenant remembered the promise of God to Abraham in Genesis 12:3, which said in Abraham all the nations of the earth would be blessed. That was in reference to the coming Messiah (the Seed of the woman, Genesis 3:15).

Jeremiah described the benefits of the new covenant relationship with God: forgiveness of sin, a new heart along with the indwelling Spirit of God. Participants would know God in a personal way. The new covenant is a glorious promise of salvation.

Conclusion

Now you have a basic vocabulary of words that will bring clarity to conversations with JGCs, as well as a collection of key concepts and how they are likely to be viewed by Jewish partners. You also have a biblical basis for discussing the original meaning of these concepts when they begin making their way into conversations. That could happen when couples begin discussing their challenges, which include religious differences. The next chapter will provide you with a tool that might prove helpful for couples to begin opening up about those challenges.

Exercise

One reason why people who are not Christians find it difficult to grasp the concepts of sin and salvation is that most are unfamiliar with the concept of holiness. Most don't know what it means to violate God's holiness, or why being made holy like Him is wholly desirable or of any benefit.

What do you think a secular Jew would say if you asked what they think it means to be holy? An Orthodox Jew?

If you can, find a few Jewish people who are willing to help you with a quick bit of research. Try to find at least one secular and one religious, and ask what they believe it means to be holy. Then ask them to tell you the source of their impression or idea of holiness.

HE SAID *then* SHE SAID

Using a concordance and/or Bible dictionary (or website), do your own study on the meaning of holiness. Then write down at least three Scriptures that describe holiness as something that an average person with no church background would find desirable.

How might holiness be a factor in finding spiritual harmony? Write your answer using words that a person with no church background will be able to understand.

1. I've written a booklet about the Hebrew concept of "conversion" called *Turning to God*, available to you at j4j.co/turningtoGod.
2. Download a free copy of an article about sin, written from a Messianic Jewish perspective, at: http://jewsforjesus.org/publications/issues/v09-n08/sin.

Chapter 4
Help with First Encounters

I want you to have a tool that has given me a good point of entry as I minister to Jewish-Gentile couples. During my first meeting with a couple, I often give them a photocopy of a chart I've developed, and ask them how their experience compares to what they see.

What It Is

I took what 52 Jewish-Gentile couples told me about their experiences and challenges during research interviews and created this chart based upon that information. The chart simply reflects the life situations and the challenges that Jewish-Gentile couples reported at various stages of their relationships.

Culture can be really hard to detect and it's nearly invisible to people who don't know what it is or how it affects them. Some people love the smell of garlic and think of it as "my kinda food." Others associate it with distasteful (sorry) olfactory overkill. Those are just cultural preferences. But when it comes to how we think things ought to be or the right way to behave, it's natural to feel tense and even judgmental when others don't see things the same way. This chart describes some of the typical cross-cultural challenges that Jewish-Gentile couples reported as their common experiences.

How It Works

The chart, or grid, begins with the left-hand column, Relational Stages. These four stages capture the categories that various couples described as stages in their relationship. You'll find more about these stages in chapters 7 through 9.

Across the top row are the five most common cultural categories where challenges reportedly popped up. These are the same challenges I listed in the introduction, as reported by participants in study surveys.

These challenges can be described as "cultural flash points of cross-cultural conflict." I'll simply refer to them as "flash points." They make it a bit easier to anticipate specific challenges, stumbling blocks or objections.

Finding where the stages of the relationships and the cultural categories intersect brings you to a box of issues or challenges that many couples identified as relevant to that stage of their relationship. For example, if you take couples who are "dating and in discovery mode," and go to "raising children" you'll find that couples dealt with such challenges as each partner's expectations concerning the identity and religion of future children, as well as what other family members expect. You can see that at this stage, the couple can try to come to an agreement about future children, or they can avoid discussing these issues.

Now look at what happens when you stay in the raising children category, but take the next step on the relationship side, which is "wedding ceremony." You can see that the details of the wedding establish a pattern for identity and religion that is likely to affect decisions about children in the future. You also see that whereas family might have had expectations or hopes concerning future children while the couple was dating, now that there's a wedding ahead, they are likely to express more definite preferences concerning what the children's identity and religion will be.

Trust builds as the couple sees others give voice to their experience and struggles without judging them.

Similarly, after the wedding and before the birth of children, expectations and preferences become pressures to make choices. And as unavoidable as such pressures may be, the couple will still have to decide whether to avoid or engage in discussing the choices they need to make. Because when it comes to avoiding discussion, as the old saying goes, "Not to decide is to decide."

The Key

I scaled the information way down to fit into the grid because there's value in seeing at what point in a relationship couples experience specific challenges. I've provided a key beginning on page 32, in case the meaning of words in any particular box is not self-evident. For the purposes of the key, each box is coded with a number and letter. The numbers, 1–4, represent the stages of relationship going down the far left column. The letters, A–E, represent the five cultural categories going across the top.

So, for example, the box coded 1D is the one containing the words *taboos, prejudices and acceptance*, which are italicized in the key. Couples used these words to describe issues arising during their dating/discovery phase. The key briefly explains what the couples meant by the italicized words and phrases.

What to Expect

I don't recommend that you attempt to have couples consult this chart for a "diagnosis" of their own relationships. Nor should you expect that it can pinpoint every challenge the couples you meet might be facing now or in the future. But when you give them a photocopy/pdf of this chart (and ask them how their experience compares to what they see) here's what is likely to happen:

- The couple realizes they are not alone.
- Trust builds as the couple sees others give voice to their experience and struggles without judging them.
- They are grateful to have an objective tool with which to examine some of their own challenges.
- As they articulate their response, you gain understanding about the issues the couple is facing.

Let me unpack that.

First, remember that many Jewish-Gentile couples have a deep sense of isolation or loneliness about their significant cross-cultural barriers. When you show this chart to couples, be sure to explain that all the information (including the categories used across the top) was gathered from other Jewish-Gentile couples. Mention the statistics regarding intermarriage from the "bit of background" in the introduction. This often comes as a great relief to JGCs. It shows them that they are not alone, that others know from experience what they are going through. Most will be surprised and appreciative to hear that they are part of a large community of other Jewish-Gentile couples in the United States today.

It shows them that they are not alone, that others know from experience what they are going through.

Second, as you explain that the chart was created in order to better understand Jewish-Gentile couples who were seeking help, you are showing that someone cared enough to take an objective look at their situation in order to understand, not to judge. As you share this information with them, it brings you into that same position of understanding and not judging. This helps create a sense of trust as well as partnership as you join with couples to help them find a way through their very complex multidimensional experience.

Your ability to see what is happening with their relationships helps to lay the foundation for trust. Creating trust, building on that trust and maintaining it are all crucial in our ability to extend spiritual ministry to Jewish-Gentile couples. Beyond that, we have to continue doing things to preserve that trust. This is the gateway to extending spiritual ministry to the Jewish-Gentile couples and their families.

Third, showing Jewish-Gentile couples the chart can give them a sense of clarity about what they are experiencing. Most are able to recognize their own situation very quickly.[1] They can see that others identified many of the flash points that they have been experiencing in their relationship. That often serves as a starting place to help them understand what's happening to them. Clarity is a comforting thing, especially when you have been living in Confusionville!

The chart drills down into specific challenges others experienced. This gives couples a more objective basis to discuss their own challenges. The couple can see that they are part of a bigger picture; it's not just a matter of their two personalities. Instead of talking about one another's shortcomings or "who's to blame" for failures to understand/communicate, couples are redirected to focus on the different perspectives and unique cultures represented within each box.

As a participant-observer, you can help couples find a safer way to discuss the life experiences represented in one or more of those squares. Utilize what you've learned about being a cross-cultural translator, and help the couples find ways to speak to, rather than at or past, one another.

Finally, looking at the chart before your first meeting with a couple will help you better understand the challenges facing JGCs; looking at it again with the couples you meet will be a time of learning more about them as individuals. Their willingness to discuss the chart can be a good time of relationship building for all concerned.

Reference Key

<u>Dating/Discovery Phase</u>

1A. Cross-cultural challenges of personal identity in the dating/discovery stage

Communication of self and hearer: couples discover that words they use to describe themselves have different meanings in their partner's culture.

Social network tensions arise as JGC partners learn about their different communal identities.

Personal religious identity is hard for dating couples to understand/discuss since they often differ about the meaning and importance of "religion."

1B. Cross-cultural challenges about religion in the dating/discovery stage

Differences regarding Judaism, Jesus and Christianity: these words and concepts have different implications or associations for each partner.

Confusion over ethnicity and belief when some partners wrongly assume beliefs are prescribed through bloodline or ethnicity.

Practices vs. beliefs: ritual practices don't always represent deeply held beliefs. Couples need to learn what meanings their partners ascribe to them.

1C. Cross-cultural challenges around life-cycle events in the dating/discovery stage

Religious events: dating couples need to set aside assumptions to discover the important religious practices in the lives of their partners.

Rituals observed: JGCs need to discover what their partner's rituals mean, why they do them, and how important it is to them to continue them.

Holiday events: couples need to ask, not assume. For example, one partner might mistakenly think that Hanukkah is "Jewish Christmas."

A SURVEY OF CROSS-CULTURAL CHALLENGES REPORTED BY JEWISH-GENTILE COUPLES AT DIFFERENT STAGES OF THEIR RELATIONSHIPS

		Cultural				
		Personal Identity	**Religion**	**Life-Cycle Events**	**Family**	**Raising Children**
Relational	**Dating/Discovery**	Communication of self and hearer Social network tensions Religious identity	Differences re: Judaism, Jesus and Christianity Confusion of ethnicity and belief Practices vs. beliefs	Religious events Rituals observed Holiday events Family practices	Taboos/prejudices and acceptance Cross-cultural differences Family network/ level of involvement	Expectations: child's identity and religion Family expectations to have children Agreement or avoidance
	Wedding Ceremony	Religious or secular Symbols: Jewish or Christian or both Family considerations: satisfaction, participation	Ceremony identity: one, dual, blend or neither Symbols: dominance, collaboration or compromise Elope or wedding event without family	Symbolic choices for couple identity Family network response to belief & rituals Family integration or fracture	Expectations, involvement, help or demands Symbol choices Competition, collaboration or rejection	Establishing identity and religion patterns for future children Family preference introduced for child's identity and religion
	Together without Children	Family network identity Couple identity	Holiday choices Religious practice: unified, blended, separate or none Symbols: harmony, compromises or none	Negotiating rites of passage, holidays, rituals and symbols Family expectations Communication: religious and ethnic	Family network: Integration or alienation of spouse/couple Cross-cultural ability of spouse Navigate celebrations	Avoid or discuss Family pressure Extended family advice or dreams
	Together with Children	Family identity Children's identity	Religious Holy Days Religious education Religious identity of children	Religious and/or ethnic life-cycle events Rituals and symbols Family network expectations	Family spiritual harmony Family identity Religious identity and family connection	Enculturation by collaboration, delegation, abdication or competition Training by intent or accident

Family practices: there's another learning curve regarding meaning of words each partner's family uses to describe their religious practices.

1D. Cross-cultural challenges about family in the dating/discovery stage
Taboos/prejudices and acceptance: discovering restrictions, prohibitions and biases in one another's families is difficult; approaching those subjects can threaten the couple's relationship.

Cross-cultural differences: partners discover they live in very different cultural worlds; distinctions are amplified when other family members are involved.

Family network level of involvement: increased involvement with JGCs families is natural as the relationship develops; it also intensifies the cross-cultural challenges.

1E. Cross-cultural challenges about raising children in the dating/discovery stage
Expectations: child's identity and religion. People tend to expect that "my child" will "believe like I do." That is a tough discussion to have between two potential parents who believe differently.

Family expectations about the couple having children: two sets of potential grandparents' differing expectations adds another set of challenges.

Agreement or avoidance: Agreement to discuss expectations regarding children sometimes heads off significant distress later, though it is no guarantee.

Wedding Ceremony
2A. Cross-cultural challenges of personal identity in the wedding ceremony stage
Religious or secular: couples need to agree on whether the ceremony will reflect their beliefs, including beliefs regarding marriage.

Symbols: every symbol has to be explained to the other person and then a joint decision has to be made.

Family considerations, satisfaction, participation: how will the couple involve parents in planning and participating; how will they balance their preferences with keeping peace in the family.

2B. Cross-cultural religious challenges in the wedding ceremony stage
Ceremony identity: the ceremony either features one religious culture as dominant, both as a dual cultural identity, or blends the two (such as two clergy co-officiating), or it will be secular with no reference to God or to His Word.

Symbols: will one culture's symbols dominate? Will there be a collaboration using both cultures' symbols (as with a JGC where both believe in Jesus) or will symbols of two distinct religions take turns in a ceremony without trying to synthesize them?

Elope or have wedding event without family: religious identity posed such irreconcilable tensions for some JGC families that the couple considered eloping; others, in unusual circumstances, chose to not have one or both families present at their ceremonies.

2C. Cross-cultural challenges of the wedding ceremony as a life-cycle event
Symbolic choices for couple identity: couples who grew up imagining their future wedding with familiar symbols were disheartened by the thought of compromising their identity.

Family network response to beliefs and rituals: when two sets of traditions vie for prominence, families may view any deviation or accommodation with disappointment and even grief.

Family integration or fracture around wedding ceremonies: couples struggled to embrace one another's cultural traditions in planning their wedding. Family members would either integrate change into their expectations or react by fracturing the family network.

2D. Cross-cultural challenges of the wedding ceremony in relationship to family
Expectations, involvement, help or demands: family responses to a JGC wedding ceremony were based on expectations about traditions "in our culture." Depending on their comfort in embracing cultural diversity in a ceremony, family members might be involved in wedding plans, help with the event or make demands.

Symbol choices are as much a source of challenge for families as they are for the couple getting married. Family preferences can add tension to already complex choices the couple is making.

Competition, collaboration or rejection: the couple often encounters a combination of these as families come together (or don't) around the wedding ceremony.

2E. Cross-cultural challenges about future children at the wedding ceremony stage
Establishing identity and religious patterns for future children: couples described added pressure/responsibility in planning their wedding ceremony, knowing wedding ceremonies set a pattern for cultural and religious identity of future children.

Family preference introduced: people are often unaware of the pressure they exert in voicing their hopes for the identity and religion of the couple's future children.

<u>Together without Children</u>
3A. Cross-cultural challenges of personal identity when a couple is together without children
Family network identity: once they are together or married without children, couples are challenged to understand their new combined cultural identity as part of a family network.

Couple identity: during this period of challenge to form a new identity, many religiously cross-cultural couples became aware of their inability to find spiritual harmony.

3B. Cross-cultural challenges of religious identity when a couple is together without children

Holiday choices have to be made thoughtfully as each partner discovers what beliefs and religious practices really matter to them.

Religious practice: JGCs navigate which religious practices will reflect their "home" culture. They may find a comfortable unified religious life, or blend elements from both cultures, or choose to practice separate beliefs individually or decide on no religion in their home.

Symbols: as with practices, symbols can be a source of cultural strain or mutual appreciation. Couples must discuss the meaning of religious symbols brought into their home to maintain peace and mutual appreciation.

3C. Cross-cultural challenges around life-cycle events when a couple is together without children

Negotiating rites of passage, holidays, rituals and symbols: thoughtful discussions and decisions are needed to combine two sets of cultural expectations and history into a new home and joint identity.

Family expectations: these can add pressure to the already challenging decisions facing JGCs.

Communication—religious and ethnic: in discussing choices, it is valuable to make a distinction between cycle celebrations or events that are either religious or national/ethnic in nature.

3D. Cross-cultural challenges happen around family influences when a couple is together without children

Family network—integration or alienation: care must be made to introduce new partners to one another's in-laws as family members who have new and different cultural understanding and expectations. Some families embrace and integrate the spouse into their network; others tend to alienate the spouse or the couple.

Cross-cultural ability of spouse: the above outcomes can be influenced by each partner's ability to relate cross-culturally to members of their new family network.

Navigate celebrations: partners need to collaborate in discussion about what is appropriate for their family celebrations.

3E. Cross-cultural challenges around raising children when a couple is together yet without them

Avoid or discuss: conversations about raising future children in a dual-culture home are likely to produce tensions. If the conversation didn't take place during the dating phase, it is best not avoided at this point.

Family pressure: members, especially parents, can unintentionally add pressure to an already challenging conversation by introducing their own hopes/expectations about future children. Extended family advice or dreams: members may also add pressure to a JGC by voicing unsolicited advice or dreams about the faith and culture of potential offspring.

Together with Children

4A. Cross-cultural challenges of personal identity when a couple has children
Family identity: arrival of children brings a new dimension to the couple, who now are challenged to define their identities as parents of a family, and make choices that will affect their children's identity.

Children's identity: this will reflect the parents' understanding of one another's cultural differences; parents decide whether the children are identified with the ethnicity and culture of one parent, a blend of both or possibly neither.

4B. Cross-cultural challenges of religious identity when a couple has children
Religious Holy Days: observances become choices about the children's enculturation. Competition or collaboration about the future identity of the children often surfaces around holidays.

Religious education: this can be a flash point between partners; also parents who have not settled how to have spiritual harmony communicate their unsettled state, even if unintentionally, to their children.

Religious identity of children: this is usually shaped in one of four methods: couples may collaborate, delegate, abdicate or compete. (See chapter 9.)

4C. Cross-cultural challenges around life-cycle events when a couple has children
Religious and/or ethnic life-cycle events: couples need to consider the appropriateness, purpose and meaning in every life-cycle event, as these all contribute to the cultural training and identity of children.

Rituals and symbols: these are a significant part in celebrating rites of passage, holidays, and identity. Parents should be aware that their choices are training their children.

Family network expectations: families can impose cultural expectations without realizing that doing so might cause a cross-cultural offense. It might be wise for couples to discuss/explain the life-cycle events of their children with both sets of parents.

4D. Cross-cultural challenges happen around family influences when a couple has children
Family spiritual harmony: the presence or absence of this impacts the lives of both parents and children. Spiritual harmony occurs when parents share a similar relationship with the one true God; that is one of the greatest challenges reported by JGCs.

Family identity: this is important for the healthy internal functioning of the Jewish-Gentile couple and their children, and if it has not been forged already, it becomes an even greater challenge when children arrive.

Religious identity and family connection: choices about religious belief and identity can have consequences in the family network.

4E. Cross-cultural challenges with enculturating children

Enculturation: as with religious identity, parents enculturate their children either by collaboration, delegation, abdication or competition.

Training: the first point of enculturation for children is in their home, and they will be trained either by intention or by accident. Partners who have found spiritual harmony together are better equipped to enculturate children intentionally.

Conclusion

You now have a tool that offers an effective means of discussion for your first meeting with a Jewish-Gentile couple. The chart can also serve as a prompt to set up that first meeting when you are in the early stages of reaching out to a couple. If one or both partners tell you a little about their situation, that is, cultural challenges they are facing, you can ask if they would find it helpful to hear what other JGCs had to say about their own challenges.

Exercise

Using the chart on p. 33 with a JGC will be, in itself, the primary exercise! Make sure that you are ready to use it:

- Be familiar enough with the chart that you can describe what it is, its origins and how it works for your first meeting.
- Make a photocopy (or two) for the couple so they can take it home with them and perhaps even highlight the boxes they are interested in discussing more.
- Familiarize yourself with the key so that if questions arise about any of the phrases in the boxes, you can easily explain the challenges they refer to.

1. Life is complex, so there are always surprises that don't necessarily fit into a chart or model like this. For example, you may meet couples that have been "dating for a long time." Though they have never been through a wedding, actually they are currently living together. Their issues are more often like those encountered by a couple that dated, married and are now together but "without children." They are trying to find individual identities and a common spiritual harmony.

Chapter 5
Opening the Bible

How do you actually get around to introducing the Bible into a conversation? Believe it or not, you already know how to get started!

You've learned about "basic vocabulary that isn't so basic" and you know how to create clarity around key words like *Christ* by first asking each partner what that words means to them. That step helps clear up misunderstandings that arise when two people use the same word but mean different things. When you present a third meaning you can say something to the effect of, "Would it be okay to take a look at what the Bible says to define the word *Christ* both from grammar and in its historical context?" You're asking permission, and taking the conversation out of the realm of subjective ideas or personal feelings.

You can do the same when moving from key words to biblical/theological concepts. After hearing each partner's take on a word like *sin* it's appropriate to say, "The Bible has an interesting perspective on this concept. Can we take a quick look and I'll show you?"

Most people will not object to learning the biblical meaning of words and concepts—it doesn't require them to agree with their meanings, or to accept the Bible as an authority on how to live their lives—it simply helps them and their partner learn to speak the same language.

The Next Step

Agreeing to consider what the Bible says about an issue or challenge the couple has acknowledged to you is a bigger step. Look for a moment in a conversation—a special moment that indicates an unbelieving partner is willing to read from the Bible. In a way they're saying, "I'm going to give God permission to speak into my life." It never happens in those words, but that's the reality.

The moment may come when a partner asks a question or makes a statement that prompts you to ask if they would like to see what the Bible has to say about the matter. A couple might talk about tension that they face because the Jewish partner's family had hoped they would choose a Jewish mate. You might offer, "It's always hard to have people we care about express doubt or disapproval of our choices. You might be surprised by what the Bible says about Jewish people 'marrying out.' Would you be open to taking a look?"

You could also respond by saying, "Yes, that's probably the Jewish survival instinct kicking in. But you know, the Bible has some interesting things to say about the survival of the Jewish people that might encourage you. Is that something you might want to explore with me?"

At the end of this chapter, you'll find a biblical survey on the subject of intermarriage that can serve as a starting place for those who might be interested. Appendix 2 is a brief look at Jewish survival from a biblical perspective. These are for you to use or modify . . . or even just see as examples of the studies you can put together if that is your gifting.

If the couple agrees to see what the Bible says about intermarriage or some other topic, suggest meeting for a set number of sessions (don't make it too many) so they know it's not an open-ended commitment.

Try to help the couple set aside preconceptions about how their partner should view the Scriptures.

When you meet, listen carefully to their questions, focus your answer on what the Bible says and err on the side of saying too little rather than too much. Asking "Does that make sense?" or "Did that answer your question?" gives others the opportunity to let you know if they are looking for more. Before you part ways, give them an assignment to consider outside of your meeting time. They may need the space to think and discuss together what they are learning from the Bible.

Avoid Presuppositions

Someone's willingness to look into the Bible with you does not mean they will accept its findings as authoritative. A Jewish partner may read the Gospel of John merely to understand the message of Jesus—to show they want to understand their partner's beliefs. That doesn't mean they are willing to know God or submit to His Word. That willingness is a supernatural work of the Holy Spirit. Part of our ministry to JGCs is to pray faithfully for that work in their lives.

In some cases you'll meet with only one partner. Other times you'll meet together with the couple. If the three of you are studying together, try to help the couple set aside preconceptions about how their partner should view the Scriptures. For example, Christians are often surprised if their Jewish partner is "biblically illiterate." Consequently I hear judgmental statements about a Jewish partner for not knowing the Bible, not owning a Bible, or simply being dismissive of the Bible.

Gently point out that such criticism doesn't help a conversation. Use the demographics at the beginning of this book to deal with stereotypes and/or unrealistic expectations about Jewish people. A Jewish partner's lack of interest much less knowledge of the Bible will not surprise someone who knows that more than two-thirds of American Jewry is disaffiliated from the synagogue or other Jewish institutions.

What about Atheists?

What do you do when somebody says he/she rejects the Bible because he/she is an atheist? First of all, try to understand what they mean; draw out the full extent of their disbelief. Atheism asserts, "There is no God." That's a pretty hard philosophy to defend. Has the person explored every possible avenue that might lead him or her to believe that God is real, and found them all to be false? Of course not!

Remember, we're just talking about belief, not proof. You could ask, "Are you certain that you've seen and known everything that can be discovered about the possible existence of God?" Most people realize there is always more to be discovered and will express doubt. I've found it sometimes helpful to say, "Are you a committed atheist, or are you really an agnostic?" The agnostic says, "There might be a God; I just don't know and I'm not sure it's possible to know." Frequently, people realize that they just don't know (and sometimes don't want to know) if God is real—yet. At that point we have a mutual understanding that discovery might be possible. The Bible can be a source for that discovery.

Permission to Quote

We who believe the Bible is God's Word have a tendency to quote it as our "go to" resource for navigating all life's challenges. Many people we'll meet and minister to don't see it that way at all. If they don't believe in God, they don't believe in a Word of God. If they do believe that God exists and that He communicated through the Bible, they might feel that the manuscripts have been so corrupted and mistranslated over the years that it's not possible to know what was originally said.

"What makes you think the Bible is anything more than a book written by ordinary people?" is a fair and honest question. How do we know the Bible is God's Word? For one thing, because the Bible says it is God's word. But—that is circular reasoning! And circular reasoning is no basis for a logical argument.

Be prepared to give at least one objective statement in defense of the Bible, and be ready to suggest a book for more information on the topic.

Numerous Christian scholars have written objectively about the Bible and its accuracy. If you don't already have a favorite among them, it would be good to find/choose one. Be prepared to give at least one objective statement in defense of the Bible, and be ready to suggest a book for more information on the topic. Only a small percentage of people will take the time to read an apologetic book about the Bible, but it doesn't hurt for people to know they exist. Remember, as with belief in God, so belief in His Word usually depends at least in part on the desire to know whether it's true.

There is subjective evidence from the impact of the gospel in each of our lives. Christian historian Kenneth S. Latourette observed there can be no doubt that Jesus' life has had more impact on the world than any other. There is the general revelation of God's creation. That, too, goes back to what the Bible says about creation, particularly in the Psalms and the book of Romans. There is special revelation in the person and the work of Jesus the Messiah, again as described in Scripture.

But how do you answer the objection that the Bible has been so changed and corrupted over time that we no longer can know its original intent?

My systematic theology professor, Dr. David Wells, gave a memorable argument that I have often used: Which was harder for God to do? Was it more difficult for Him to send His Son as Savior to sacrifice His life as an act of love for human beings? Or was it more difficult to write a historically accurate statement to preserve the truth of what that sovereign God has done? Reasonable people generally can see the answer to that question. It was certainly harder to do the salvation thing than to write a report of it.[1]

Jesus cautioned against putting truth in front of people who are unable to appreciate it. He used culturally appropriate imagery for His time and context. He essentially said, "Don't try and show a pig the beauty of a pearl." The poor piggy has no ability to appreciate the aesthetic beauty of jewelry. Perhaps with a twinkle in His eye, Jesus knew that the pig was more likely to eat the pearl than to appreciate it.

Keep in mind that Jewish and other Asian cultures preferred word pictures or stories to convey concepts. So, don't presume that Jesus was saying someone who doesn't know or accept the Bible is a stupid pig. I just want to get that out of the way. He simply wants us to be discerning about who is or isn't ready for the treasure offered in His Word.

Discussing the Text

Since one or both partners might not necessarily know the Bible or agree to the authority of its content, you can let the study partners know that they don't have to agree to the authority of the Bible in order to explore what it has to say. I believe that God ultimately holds all of us accountable for what we do with the revelation of Scripture. But I am free to commend what the Bible says without laying that burden on people, especially when they are willing to look at the Scriptures out of simple curiosity.

Introducing a Bible text into a discussion with Jewish-Gentle couples brings a fourth culture to the conversation. God communicated through the mind, personality and writing instrument of the human author. In order to communicate God's intended meaning, we have to be aware of the cultural understandings of both partners.

As with key words and concepts, we need to ask and listen, back and forth, to each of their traditional views about the Bible passage. You listen to what they perceive a passage to mean; translate between them and then let them hear what the text has to say. When it comes to that last step, I prefer to let the text speak for itself. For more on this subject see, "Let the Text Speak for Itself" at http://www.gospel-life.net/let-the-text-speak-for-itself/.

As mentioned, the unique challenges JGCs face might open the opportunity to suggest the following as a basis for opening the Scriptures:

What does the Bible say about Jews marrying people from other nations?

Is it permitted or is it totally forbidden?

Is the chief concern that children of intermarriage will no longer be Jewish?

How important is it that a couple shares the same religion?

Does the Bible say the Jewish intermarriage is a threat to ethnic survival? If not, what if any threat is there?

The Bible is clear concerning the Lord's chief concern when it comes to intermarriage. His covenant, to preserve the seed of Abraham like the stars of heaven, was realized by Jewish participation in that promise through faith. Their peril was focused on a potential abandonment of faith that resulted from intermarriage with ungodly peoples.

The Bible offers support for this poignant spiritual threat. I've compiled a brief biblical survey on intermarriage as appendix 3. It will be helpful for you to review it as a background to your discussions with couples, even if they choose not to look at the passages with you. The material will inform and enable you to discuss various concerns about intermarriage, which ones might be valid and which are not.

Conclusion

Remember, patience and prayer go a long way in opening opportunities for Bible discussions. You'll be able to put the principles you've learned here into practice in God's good timing.

Exercise

Think through and list five things you can say about the Bible that might appeal to those who are unfamiliar with it and/or do not accept it as authoritative.

How might a discussion/study about intermarriage differ when interacting with a dating couple as opposed to a married couple?

As you compare and contrast marital prohibitions/admonitions in the Bible, keep in mind God's purpose. Now write one impactful sentence describing that purpose in a way that could be meaningful to JGCs.

1. David F. Wells, *No Place for Truth: Or Whatever Happened to Evangelical Theology?* (Grand Rapids: William B. Eerdmans Publishing Company, 1993).

Chapter 6
Getting to the Gospel

Opportunities to discuss the gospel will arise in Jewish-Gentile ministry, especially as the hope of spiritual harmony is raised. If you don't have a lot of experience with gospel conversations, this chapter has a whole lot to offer. Don't feel the need to process it all at once!

First, it's important for couples to know that when you talk about finding spiritual harmony, you don't mean becoming more religious.

It's All about Relationships

Spiritual harmony happens when we connect with the One who made us and is best able to help us understand ourselves and others. It's learning to see a truth that's bigger and brighter than our own individual opinions and preferences. That truth has room for—but is not limited or defined by—individual cultures.

I believe that any couple can find spiritual intimacy when each partner independently seeks to know God.

Couples long for a spiritual connection that reaches to the core of who they are. God designed us to have that kind of intimacy with Him, and when both partners experience that intimacy with Him it provides a strong foundation for intimacy with each other. This is what you want the people you are serving to understand.

When people receive God's grace and forgiveness through Jesus, something amazing happens. They extend grace and forgiveness to others. They connect on a heart level with others who've had the same experience.

Jewish-Gentile couples have very different identities stemming from ethnicity and enculturation. But when a dynamic relationship with God becomes central to both their identities, a new and grace-filled culture emerges, enabling them to navigate their differences.

To Seek or Not to Seek

Some people seek God because they are in pain and nothing else has helped. Others want to know God because they see qualities in others who know Him, qualities they want in their own hearts and lives. But it's important to remember that many aren't seeking God and don't see any reason to.

I stated at the outset of this book that I believe the gospel is the only way to have a personal relationship with God. I also mentioned that, as open as I am about my beliefs, I don't find it necessary to begin the relationship with a gospel conversation—and neither should you.

I believe that any couple can find spiritual intimacy when each partner independently seeks to know God.

If our hope is that each partner will independently seek to know God, we have to ask, how does that happen? What does it look like? Chances are, it won't begin with someone wanting to know all about Jesus. A first step toward seeking is for people to realize that they need to be open to God in a way that He chooses to be known. Another, harder way to say this is that people don't get to choose how to have a relationship with God—just by virtue of the fact that God is God and we aren't.

Seeking God means being open to how He chooses to reveal Himself. Seeking God also includes wanting to know what He wants for us and from us.

Many people are not open to knowing God for those very reasons. What if God chooses to reveal something we've committed ourselves to ignoring? What if what God wants isn't always the same as what we want? These are uncomfortable possibilities. Many find it easier to think of God as being too distant to take a personal interest in us.

And yet we can't get away from the fact that what we think (or don't think) about God is an important part of who we are. If He is the creator, then to know Him is to know and fulfill our purpose and potential. That's powerful. It's worth the risk of seeking God on His terms.

If a person is willing to seek God, what can they do?

Encourage people to start by asking God questions. Let them know it's okay to be skeptical and that many prayers begin with "God, if you're there . . ."

The question "Who are You and how am I doing?" is a good first step. It requires some vulnerability, but that is an important part of seeking. The next question is, "How can I know You?"

I believe that whoever sincerely asks God, "How can I know You?" will find the answer in Jesus. But how a person arrives at that sincere desire, or even how long it takes for God to answer that desire, is a mystery.

Which brings us to this: Where does your part of the gospel conversation come in?

At the end of this chapter I'll give examples of how to engage in gospel conversations as opportunities arise.

How do I know when and how much to discuss the gospel?

The best and most in-depth gospel conversations usually take place in the context of a trusted relationship. Building that trust might take a lot of time or a little time.

Gospel conversations don't necessarily take place during your "ministry hours." They might take place while you're simply walking to get a cup of coffee. I have a Jewish friend who loves to discuss the most personal questions of life while on a hike. As you develop a listening ear, you will recognize cues, both from the people you want to share with, as well as from the Holy Spirit.

Remember that a gospel conversation is not a matter of downloading information. It's a partnership between you, God and the people who want to know Him. It's not our job to make sure that a person understands everything at once and is ready to act on what they've heard.

In fact, overcommunication actually undermines communication. If somebody asks you a question with enough interest to fill a thimble, don't give a "two-gallon answer." You could drown their enthusiasm for truth. It is better to answer briefly, then ask, "Does that make sense?" or "Is it answering your question?" If they are dissatisfied and/or looking for more, then you are probably doing your job!

By the way, you should not be surprised if you get some angry feedback as you explain the gospel. This is not necessarily a red light to further conversation; in fact, it can actually be a positive sign. (See why in appendix 5.)

Levels of Interest

You'll most likely encounter three different levels of interest that can lead to gospel conversations.

> *If somebody asks you a question with enough interest to fill a thimble, don't give a "two-gallon answer."*

1. Simple curiosity

This is not a particularly personal interest. Some people just wonder what Christians believe. With Jewish-Gentile couples, even if one partner is a Christian, don't be surprised if the other does not know what Christianity is all about. She or he may have heard snatches that were too culturally foreign to understand. Or the message might have been delivered with emotional baggage that obscured the meaning.

2. Desire to understand one's partner

This is a little more personal; it's motivated by a need to understand a loved one. But for the reasons stated above, that understanding can be elusive. Partners who have been unsuccessful in communicating their beliefs may withdraw from further attempts—especially if the unsuccessful attempts ended in a heated or hurtful exchange.

Neither of these two levels is likely to lead a person to respond to the gospel message in faith. Our goal is to create understanding about the message of Messiah Yeshua.

Many people think of sin as a crime punishable by our legal system, and don't see themselves as sinners at all.

With that in mind, you should be able to explain the message of the gospel so that anyone, including Jewish people, can understand it in their own cultural frame of reference.

While you don't want to respond to mere curiosity with a disproportionately long speech, a thoughtful explanation takes something more than an elevator pitch. In other words, you probably need more than 30 seconds to get the message across! You'll want to communicate the core issues of the gospel:

God desires to have a loving and dynamic relationship with the people He created.

Our sin separates us from God, resulting in physical and spiritual death.

God made it possible for us to be reconciled to Him through Jesus, who, by His death, took the punishment we deserve, and by His resurrection showed that God has not only judged sin and death, but has broken its power.

By agreeing with God about our sin, turning from it and receiving the forgiveness Jesus made possible, we are reconciled to God and empowered to know and enjoy Him in this life and the next.

I've stated these issues in a way that is familiar to you as a Christian, but you will need to communicate them in different words to someone who is not familiar with the concepts. I'll let you know what works for me in the section Gospel Steps: Understanding Four Realities.

You might find that sections of the gospel come out in one conversation at a time. For example, it may or may not be appropriate to begin with God's love and desire for a relationship with us. Someone who is unsure that God exists or simply is not interested in God will not be able to appreciate that. That person might need to first hear about the barrier that keeps people from knowing God—that has disabled us from even wanting to know Him. And though Christians know that barrier as sin, that word has very limited meaning to most people. It probably won't help to say, "Your sin is separating you from God." Many people think of sin as a crime punishable by our legal system, and don't see themselves as sinners at all.

3. Personal Realization

A third level of interest leading to gospel conversations is when a person is aware of their spiritual need to know God. They are ready to receive, know and, by faith, believe the truth.

The person may or may not realize they are at that point. They will have realized a need for spiritual truth but may not have processed what it would mean to receive it. Sometimes it is appropriate to ask, "Are you ready to trust God?" Another way to ask is, "If you could know what God wants for you and from you, would you be willing to believe and follow through even if there were social consequences?" You might phrase the question differently, but be ready to ask. This kind of question not only helps you discern the level of interest; it might actually help the person to recognize their own growing desire and willingness to receive what God shows them.

When you sense that someone is at this third stage of interest in the gospel, it is not just a matter of informing her of what we believe. It's a matter of how this might apply to her own situation.

Questions to Help You Connect

Is there anything you can do to encourage that process toward their openness? Sure, ask meaningful and engaging questions when given the opportunity to explore life issues more deeply.

Ask what they believe about God. Listen carefully and patiently.

Ask how they know their belief about God might be true. Did they learn about God from their parents, family, rabbi, personal experience or . . . ? How do they know what they believe is true? (Be prepared to answer that question for your own faith as well!)

Focus on listening to the other person's spiritual ideas, cultural signals and the meaning of their words. When you listen with the intent of truly learning about the other person, windows to gospel conversations open very naturally.

When it's appropriate, ask questions like, "If God is real, what would you want Him to do for you?" Be prepared for the other person to ask you to answer the same question—or even to respond, "Why should God do anything for me?" And don't be put off if they should reply with something like, "Oh, nothing really. I'm not even sure that God is there." At that point you might want to explore what they do or don't believe about God.

Ask meaningful and engaging questions when given the opportunity to explore life issues more deeply.

You can also ask, "If God is real, what do you think He wants from you?" Here again, it is sort of a "what if" question that can prime the pump for further conversation.

Similarly, I've encouraged countless people to pray, "Lord, I don't know You, but I'm asking You, please show me who You are and help me to see what I am like in Your eyes." I've even written out that prayer so the person I'm sharing with can pray it in a private moment. I've also added a disclaimer I've actually used in my own prayers: "Lord, please don't scare me!"

I sometimes offer to pray that God would answer a person's heart's desire. If I offer to do that, I'll ask if it is okay to do it in his or her presence or later. I want them to know that I'm glad to pray for them, but not in a way to manipulate or make them uncomfortable.

If we want people to understand that they have a problem with sin, we need to use terms that they understand and can relate to.

These are fair questions to ask of either a Jewish or Gentile partner. Sometimes it's helpful for them to hear one another's responses. It may create more questions, but it can also lead to deeper understanding of their cross-cultural differences.

Gospel Steps: Understanding Four Realities

When explaining the gospel, I think in terms of four realities I want a person to recognize in his or her own life. Consider the level of interest to determine how much or how deeply to speak of these things. Explaining what Christians believe to someone who is merely curious will be much different than presenting these realities to someone who is actually seeking to know God.

You might express the same realities in different words, but these are mine: moral brokenness, the dilemma, the possible solution and the next step.

Moral Brokenness

If we want people to understand that they have a problem with sin, we need to use terms that they understand and can relate to. Evidence for sin is found in lots of human experiences. Sometimes it's helpful to discuss those experiences that people can relate to before explaining a theological term that might otherwise sound irrelevant.

I find that people usually grasp the fact that moral brokenness and selfishness are universal character traits that we all experience to some degree. I often use those words when beginning to explain the problem of sin. You might have similar words that mean the same thing. It's important for people to know that sin is not merely a wicked deed. It's an underlying reality that causes people to act in destructive and hurtful ways.

People experience sin's effects in many ways:

- brokenness
- regrets
- fears
- unfulfilled longings
- a sense of hopelessness from a repeated pattern of failure or disappointments
- a sense of impending doom where we can only strive for momentary snatches of happiness before something bad happens

All of these are evidence that things are not as they should be. All of these point to the problem of sin.

People seem to understand, at least from my conversations, that God was acting out of great love when He created human beings to have a fully operational free will. Amazingly, that act of love is what enables us to turn from God, as though He does not exist, or as though He is less competent than we are to rule the universe He created. Actor and producer Kindred Sheppard (born S. Abraham Sheppard) describes our common human state as having pulled the plug: our earbud connection to God has gone dead. We've chosen to live without seeking our Creator's guidance. The result is our morally dysfunctional state.

That state causes insecurities, frustrated expectations, a cycle of disappointments and a pattern of regrets. Sin leads to a dark path of confusion about why we suffer these things. Attempts to relieve that suffering are often destructive to ourselves or others. Attempts to alleviate the symptoms do not address the root cause of our brokenness. If we do look beyond the symptoms, most of us are pretty sure that the cause is rooted in someone else—not in us. If we have failed, we reason, it's because others have failed us. That's moral brokenness.

Confession is agreeing with God about what we're like, and it is not only good for the soul, it's the first step to receiving His light.

The Dilemma

Moral brokenness leads to a dilemma. When people have turned away from the light, everything is dark. A committed agnostic once told me, "I know there's a God because I can see His light from my own shadow. Y'know, I'm just more focused on my shadow."

Dwelling in darkness, separated from God, it's difficult to trust others. What would they think if they truly knew how selfish we are? Sometimes we don't even trust ourselves to see our true character. While everyone wants to be loved and secure, we can't see the only One who knows everything about us and yet truly loves us. Only He knows how we ought to function best. And yet God won't violate our freedom to make selfish choices in our dark isolation. Therein is the dilemma. God won't invade our darkness and we can't see a way out.

A Solution

The Bible suggests a way out, first by agreeing with God about our moral condition. Confession is agreeing with God about what we're like, and it is not only good for the soul, it's the first step to receiving His light.

Second, we refuse to be satisfied with our morally broken status and we turn away from that path. That's what the Bible calls *repentance*. But after turning from that destructive path, what do we turn to?

Third, recognizing that we can't fix ourselves, we face the choice to trust in someone else. We look around and realize that expecting other people to fix us would be like the proverbial blind leading the blind. Just as we can only know God as He chooses to be known, so the only solution to our brokenness is to be restored by God's grace, and by trusting in His provision.

Here you'll want to explain the gospel solution if you haven't already. God sent His Son to do for us what we cannot do for ourselves. Jesus lived a sinless life, then died in our place, taking the judgment for our sin upon Himself. The solution to our brokenness and separation from God is to receive forgiveness on His terms, trusting that His solution, Jesus, is the only one that will work. When we trust Jesus, we not only receive God's forgiveness, He gives us a new heart and a new outlook. He transforms and empowers us to be more like Jesus, yet also more like the unique individuals He created us to be. If you are speaking with a Jewish person, you'll want to be sure they understand the Jewish context of Jesus' mission. Messianic prophecies, and particularly the suffering servant passage of Isaiah 53, as well as the new covenant in Jeremiah 31, are helpful.

Recognizing that we can't fix ourselves, we face the choice to trust in someone else.

The person might not be ready to trust Jesus then and there. The following questions can help: What if the good news is true? There we are, cut off from our Creator and His light and life. No help, no hope on the side of the road that leads to spiritual death. What could possibly be the risk in asking if God really does love us enough to hear us, enough to make a way for us to know and love Him?

Next Spiritual Step

Someone who is seeking and longing to know the light welcomes help to take the next step—which is to ask God to open the door so we might see the light and know Him. Jesus said,

> So I say to you, ask, and it will be given to you; seek, and you will find; knock, and it will be opened to you. For everyone who asks receives, and he who seeks finds, and to him who knocks it will be opened. (Luke 11:9–10)

When you see that a person understands the gospel, ask if they believe it. If they say they are uncertain, ask them if they have a sense of what it would take for them to believe. You can offer to pray with them or for them to hear from God. If they say they believe, the question is, "Is there anything that would prevent you from receiving God's solution for sin and His gift of new life?"

If the person is unable to act on what they believe, hopefully they can tell you why, and you can make it a matter of prayer. But what if they are ready?

The Prayer

When the Holy Spirit is at work in someone's heart, they will not only be convinced of the truth of the gospel, they will be ready to turn to God and ask for forgiveness through His Son Jesus. They will be ready for Him to "be God" in their lives. They will need to speak frankly to God about this, praying to receive Him into their life on His terms. Christians often refer to this as "the sinner's prayer," or "a prayer for salvation."

Sometimes people will pray this on their own, from a copy of a prayer in a book or piece of gospel literature—or they might be invited to pray a similar prayer at a local congregation if they have been attending one. Then again, they might be spiritually astute enough to intuitively know what to pray on their own once they are ready to do so. But it could be that they will need your help to know how to take this step.

In case you have not done it before, here are some points to pray with a person who is professing faith in Yeshua/Jesus (use His Hebrew or English name, depending on what the person you pray with finds more natural) for the very first time:

- Lord, You are right. I am at my core selfish, and I have been in rebellion against You.
- My brokenness, my sin, has separated me from You.
- Thank You for paying the price for my offense to You when You died for me through Yeshua/Jesus on the cross.
- I am grateful that You brought Him back from the dead to show everyone that His sacrifice was sufficient for all sin and throughout all time.
- Now, as Your child, I depend on You to help me to be all that You created me to be, to grow in knowing and enjoying You, and to learn to give You the place You deserve in my life.
- In the name of Messiah, Yeshua/Jesus, amen.

It's important for that person to tell someone immediately about what they've just done, so after the prayer encourage them to make a phone call to let someone else know about it. This helps the new believer confirm what they may have done quietly in private.

Of course if you are praying with someone in the presence of their Christian partner or spouse, the phone call won't be necessary! It is an amazing joy to see a couple united in spiritual harmony and mutual intimacy with our Creator.

How Long Will It Take for a Person to Respond to Jesus?

I appreciate the Spirit's fruit of patience in the process of "making disciples." People don't enter eternal life because of our evangelistic gifts or Bible teaching abilities. It takes the Holy Spirit's work in their hearts! We get to partner with Him, which is why making disciples is such an exciting adventure with the Lord!

Patience is used to describe God: "The LORD, the LORD, a God merciful and gracious, slow to anger, and abounding in steadfast love and faithfulness (Exodus 34:6–7 ESV). "Slow to anger" or patience is translated from the Hebrew *erekh appayim*. The picture is of a king who, when provoked, inhales with flared nostrils and then holds that breath before He speaks. That describes the patience of the Lord God of Israel.

Our loving God is evidently in no hurry to judge sinners. His patient nature and kindness "leads you to repentance" (see Romans 2:4). We, who are Jesus' disciples, need the Holy Spirit to produce His fruit of patience in us if we hope to introduce others to Him.

My favorite story of God's patience (next to His patience with me!) is about Simeon, a Romanian son of Holocaust survivors. Simeon began attending the Los Angeles Jews for Jesus Bible study in the late 1980s. It was his habit to interrupt frequently and constantly ask hard philosophical questions. At times, he could be a real *nudnick* (Yiddish for a persistent bother or pest).

Simeon would constantly ask, "How do you know that really happened?" Or, "What proof do you have outside of the Bible that such a person ever lived?" Sometimes, we had to ask him to save his questions until after the Bible study just so we could get through the material for everyone else in attendance.

He was just as difficult in personal visits. Every new missionary was assigned to visit with Simeon. He was a good introduction to the difficult nature of Jewish evangelism. His tough, peppery questions seasoned new missionaries quickly. They drove us to pray for God to give us patience in the process of making disciples.

A few years ago, Simeon went through a spiritual change. After more than two decades of questioning, he no longer doubted the Bible, or even the messiahship of Jesus. He also realized his own broken, sinful humanity. However, intellectual integrity wouldn't let him fake belief in God. He had been a committed atheist. He couldn't imagine how he could just turn to have faith. With deep skepticism, he would often ask me, "How can anyone have real faith when you can't see God or the proof of His forgiveness?"

I did my best to explain that faith is a gift from God. I urged him to ask God for the blessing of faith. For two months, Simeon would ask me after every Bible study, "When is God going to answer my prayer for faith?" I had absolutely no idea, but I was confident in the patience of God's Spirit. I could tell Simeon that God would give Him faith at a time of His choosing.

On May 15, 2013, I'd prepared a Bible study on Matthew chapter 16. Usually, anywhere from 10–15 people attended the small study. Amazingly, no one showed up that night—except for Simeon. I was a little disappointed, but realized that God might have a purpose in my preparing a Bible study for one person.

Matthew 16:13–17 is the passage where Jesus asked His disciples, "Who do you say that I am?" Simon Peter answered, "You are the [Messiah] the Son of the living God." Jesus replied, "Flesh and blood has not revealed this to you, but My Father who is in heaven" (Matthew 16:17).

Simeon sat up and said, "Oh, faith is a gift that God gives people!" I paused, looking at him in amazement. Simeon finally got it! He immediately wanted to thank God for giving him the gift of faith. With his mouth he confessed, "Jesus is Lord." Simeon believed that God had raised Jesus from the grave after His death on the cross to pay for his sins. I was astonished. The process of God's patience had won the day and Simeon's heart, and it had only taken nearly 25 years!

God can be patient for as long as He chooses as He waits for the repentant sinner to turn. We may not know how long that will be, but then we aren't in charge of the discipleship process, are we?

Recognizing Opportunities for Gospel Conversations

Opportunities for gospel conversations can pop up at any time. They might come in the form of an offhand remark, a pronouncement or even a complaint from one of the partners. Often, though certainly not always, people make casual remarks to justify a lack of interest in God, albeit unconsciously. Often a simple acknowledgment followed by a question transforms these remarks, statements or even complaints into a good opportunity for a gospel conversation. Sometimes a bit of elaboration between the affirmation and the question is helpful. Even if it doesn't lead to a gospel conversation, it can cause a person to stop and reexamine their position.

The acknowledgment is important because the other person needs to know she or he has been heard. The acknowledgement is your opportunity to validate what the other person is feeling.

Your question then allows the other person to see possibilities beyond their remark, statement or complaint.

Often a simple acknowledgment followed by a question transforms these remarks, statements or even complaints into a good opportunity for a gospel conversation.

Examples:

Statement: There are so many different religions, it would be impossible to know which is true.

Affirmation: That's a good point. I'd certainly find the task of examining every single religion overwhelming, if not impossible. I don't even know how many religions exist in the world. But let me ask you . . .

Possible Questions:

Do you view knowing the truth about all religions as a prerequisite to knowing the truth about God? (Follow up with another question: Why do you/don't you think so?)

Or

If you could know the truth about God without examining every religion, would you want to?

(Again, depending on how open the person is to continuing the conversation, you might follow up with why or why not).

Statement: It's so intolerant/arrogant for Christians to think anyone that does not believe like they do is going to hell.

Affirmation: I agree that for anyone, Christian or otherwise, to say, "You have to accept my beliefs to go to heaven," would be terribly arrogant and intolerant.

Elaboration: And I feel terrible if any Christian has ever said as much to you. I only want people to believe it if it's true, and the fact that I believe it is not what makes it true. But can I ask you a question?

Questions should always be a sincere invitation for someone to share their ideas with you, not just a way for you to be able to insert your own.

Question: Do you know why Christians think that people need Jesus to have a relationship with God?

If they say yes, see if they would mind answering this: So if you were a Christian and I wasn't, what would you tell me about Jesus?

If they say no, (which is more likely) you can ask, "Would you like to know why?"

The person might say no, and then it's time to change the subject. When they see you are not going to push it, they may come back later and say, "Actually I do want to know why Christians think that."

But the person might also say yes, which is your opportunity to explain the gospel.

Depending on what kind of relationship you have with the person, there are many things in popular culture that can also lead to gospel discussions. Many book and movie themes touch on redemption and can open doors to gospel conversations. Whether it's something as classic as *Les Miserables*, or as fleetingly trendy as the *Hunger Games*, or as relevant as a current news story where someone risks their life to save another, if it comes up in conversation, you might have the opportunity to remark how deeply people are touched by stories of one person laying down their life to save another and see where the conversation goes.

Pray that God will make you aware of opportunities. If He is leading, you won't have to force a conversation; you can just put out a feeler and see if the other person is willing to engage. Questions are a good way to engage people, but make sure they are not leading questions that would back someone into a corner in order to make your point. Questions should always be a sincere invitation for someone to share their ideas with you, not just a way for you to be able to insert your own.

Conclusion

Congratulations on finishing the lengthiest chapter in this workbook! This was pivotal! If most of this information was new to you, be patient with yourself. It probably will take a while before you have most of the suggestions at your fingertips, ready to put into action. You might choose the sections you find most useful for special attention and review.

Exercise

Hope for spiritual harmony can be found when the two JGC partners are seeking the God of Abraham, Isaac and Jacob in the way that He chooses to be known.

Using the principles of asking relevant questions, how might you respectfully respond to someone who says, "I have my own path to God"?

I referenced Luke 11:9–10 to show what Jesus promised seekers. Can you add any other encouraging promises for seekers from the Hebrew Scriptures (Old Testament)?

Chapter 7
Dating Stage

Dating is a time of discovery for any couple. When it's a Jewish-Gentile couple, one thing they are likely to discover is how much they don't know about each other's culture!

I love to tell a story about Gail,* a Christian college student who didn't know any Jewish people until she caught the attention of a Jewish guy on campus.

After one of their first dates, she wanted to reciprocate his interest and for her, that meant inviting him to her church. He was confused, but composed himself and said, "I'm . . . Jewish!" She didn't hear the unspoken part of the statement, which was, "And we don't do church!"

In all earnestness, she responded, "Oh, but you would love my church. Our pastor is such a wonderful teacher." Her response didn't make sense to him and he was getting uncomfortable. "But, I'm Jewish," he repeated. She had no idea what that had to do with her church or how wonderful her pastor was.

She continued to explain more reasons why her church meant so much to her—the warmth of the congregation, for example, and their love for Jewish people. The idea of being loved by people he didn't know—and simply because he was Jewish, no less—did not make the offer any more appealing.

They were both speaking English, but neither of them understood what the other was saying. She wanted him to understand that getting to know her meant realizing how important her faith was to her.

Gail prayed for him and hoped that somehow the spiritual barrier would come down. Their relationship ended shortly after that, but God's work in the life of that Jewish college student didn't.

I know, because I was that guy.

I shared my story decades later at a missions conference. I explained that though Gail's best effort seemed to fail, God had His hand on my life and heard her prayers.

Little did I know that I was speaking at Gail's home church! After the service, she introduced herself along with her 20-year-old daughter. What a great joy that was! I'm grateful for Gail's faithfulness and God's answer to her prayers.

A Cry for Help

While this book is about ministry to Jewish-Gentile couples, I often find that I'm approached by individuals, usually Christians, who are seeking counsel. They are not yet committed to a life partner and they recognize that they have some important choices to make.

Asking a provocative question sometimes gets them thinking about the implications of their relationship.

What can you say to a young man who is dating a Jewish woman who does not yet share his faith in Messiah Jesus? A couple in love is often thinking of intimacy in a fairly narrow perspective. Asking a provocative question sometimes gets them thinking about the implications of their relationship. For example, "You are able to speak to the Lord about the deepest and most private corners of your life. Can you share what the Lord is telling you about those vulnerable places with someone who doesn't know Him?"

I have also asked, "Is this beautiful Jewish woman/man able to pray with you? Could she/he worship your Savior with you, or eventually join in raising your children to love your Savior and theirs?"

Again, dating is a time of discovery. And Jewish-Gentile couples are not only discovering things about one another, they are discovering things about themselves. You can help in that process by asking questions that will help them to really search their hearts, as mentioned above and also in chapter 6.

These questions can lead people to the kind of introspection and prayer that will move them out of a relationship. But that won't always be the case. For example . . .

Ann was a Christian and a highly trained nurse. She was in her mid-thirties when she contacted my office, seeking help in sharing her faith with Marty, a Jewish attorney about her age. Both had chosen not to pursue romance while each attended grad schools, piled up debt and then worked hard to pay down the school loans. They had met their professional and financial goals by the time they met one another and fell in love. They both wanted to marry before they got any older—but Ann had reservations about marrying someone who didn't share her faith.

We talked a few times about the potential consequences of them marrying while he did not share her faith in Jesus. She decided to take a break and allow the relationship to cool down. I actually asked her to write a brief article for my work so she could share her life lessons with others. When several months passed and I hadn't heard from her, I sent an email to check in. She wrote back to say that she hadn't written the article because she and Marty got back together and would soon marry.

Two years later, I received a note from Ann with a plaintive prayer request for Marty. They had a healthy baby, but he was troubled by the fact that she was still a Christian and likely to share her faith with their child.

People sometimes make choices that will potentially result in protracted and mutual pain. We have to be willing to stand by them through those seasons. Personal pain is a perfect teacher. I will never knowingly invite that tutor into my life, but I will stand by those who suffer its lessons. You never know when a heart will turn and open up to the Lord's ministry.

It requires the grace of God to stand with people and love them as Jesus loves them. We can't do it in our own strength, but I have repeatedly seen Him provide those resources. I trust the Lord. I believe that spiritually serving these couples is His ministry. We can count on Him in all our ways to make our paths straight. Perhaps one day I will be allowed to see Marty come to the same saving faith that sustains Ann, and hopefully, their daughter. The Holy Spirit can create understanding of His plan and give them spiritual harmony in their hearts.

"Missionary Dating"

I want to give some attention to what some people have referred to as "missionary dating." That term refers to some Christians who become romantically involved with those who don't share their faith with the intent of seeing them change. While telling themselves and maybe their friends and family that they would never marry anyone who is not a Christian, they continue along a romantic path—hoping the other person will embrace Christ before the path reaches its destination.

Personal pain is a perfect teacher. I will never knowingly invite that tutor into my life, but I will stand by those who suffer its lessons.

Such an approach is really unfair. I have asked people to imagine how they would feel if they discovered that their partner was secretly thinking, "I could never marry a Christian but I hope that I can influence him/her to give up Jesus." That reality check can help people recognize and reevaluate any hidden agendas they may have.

Jewish partners can easily be confused by those who show a romantic interest in them while also hoping to introduce Jesus into their relationship. Everyone understands romantic attraction, or *eros*. However, it's much harder to grasp the concept of the agape love of a Christian who seeks the best for another without consideration for one's own interests.

There is potential confusion for believers as well. Eros is by nature self-interested. It is passion that's guided by being loved and the accompanying feelings. Such love can obscure the selfless love of the gospel.

The hope that getting close to someone will make it possible to lead him or her to faith often backfires. Heightened emotions might continue feeding that hope, even when there's no indication that it is based on reality. Letting go of the relationship becomes more and more difficult, even as the disappointment of not being on the same page spiritually becomes deeper and more painful.

"Missionary dating" aside, by the time JGCs are ready to meet with someone for help, the relationship is usually pretty serious. Which is why . . .

Jewish-Gentile couples' ministry can be messy.

Many Christians find themselves disregarding the clear teaching of the Scriptures when it comes to romance, becoming what the Scriptures refer to as "unequally yoked" (2 Corinthians 6:14). A simple attraction can quickly turn into an intensely romantic relationship, in some cases leading to sex and the powerful emotional bonding that comes with it—again, contrary to the biblical order of things.

As the initial excitement of the relationship settles down, Christian partners often find themselves struggling to find Bible-based spiritual harmony within their own hearts as well as with their partners. That may seem strange since they chose not to be guided by Scripture when entering the relationship, but remember, the Bible includes many examples of godly people who "lapsed" for a time. It should come as no surprise that this still happens.

They do not want to be judged. And they expect that they will be in traditional religious settings.

Meanwhile, the Jewish partner is likely to be confused as spiritual concerns that weren't raised at the outset of the relationship begin to surface.

Where to Begin

Like I said, it can be messy. But a couple's desire for help once they realize the challenges facing them opens a door for ministry. That is where we encounter many couples. They do not want to be judged. And they expect that they will be in traditional religious settings.

The goal is to create understanding, so how do we begin? If we announce that they are in sin, we might as well not even start the conversation. I am not suggesting that we affirm unbiblical behavior. Should we be candid about the pitfalls of being "unequally yoked?" Absolutely! In the context of grace, and at the right time. By the way, I do not perform weddings between believers in Jesus and those who don't know Him—but I will participate in conversations about their needs.

I'll share an email I received, and an example of the kind of candid but caring response you can offer if you know someone in a similar position.

> Hello, my name is Danielle. I am a Christian who is in love with a Jewish man. My parents told me I either choose God or the Jewish man. Because marrying him would be turning my back on God. I really want him to find Christ and see the truth. But I have no clue where to start. He speaks Hebrew, French, and a good bit of English. I knew if anyone could help, ya'll [Jews for Jesus] could. I am desperate for guidance. Thanks and God bless.

My response:

Hi Danielle,

My name is Tuvya Zaretsky. I am a Jewish believer in Jesus as is my wife Ellen. I serve with Jews for Jesus in Los Angeles and since I specialize in working with Jewish-Gentile couples, your email was forwarded to me.

I began doing research into the challenges Jewish-Gentile couples face so that I could better understand the growing number of Jewish-Gentile couples contacting our office. As one result, I launched the website at http://www.JewishGentileCouples.com. You might find some helpful articles there.

From your brief description, your boyfriend sounds like he might have lived in Israel. Our ministry has a branch based in Tel Aviv; if your boyfriend is interested, here is the link to our Hebrew website: http://www.jewsforjesus.co.il/. He can browse resources in Hebrew or connect with Israelis to answer questions he might have.

Danielle, in one sense your parents have a point. No matter who you take as a husband, you will join with him in oneness (Genesis 2:24). God's ideal for marriage is intimacy that is physical, emotional and spiritual. One of the greatest challenges reported by Jewish-Gentile couples was their inability to find spiritual harmony. Christian partners often reported a deep loneliness due to their intimacy with someone who did not share their deepest belief. Their anguish for the spiritual state of their loved one was intense. Spiritual harmony can't happen until both partners know God through His only route of salvation (John 14:6).

I'm grateful to hear that you want your boyfriend to find Christ (our Messiah). Honestly, you can be a better witness to the truth if you do not have a personal stake in his response to the gospel. If you marry him, you would signal that faith in Jesus doesn't matter that much to you. And yet, I believe you love Jesus very much. Otherwise you would not reach out looking for help.

I know that these might be hard things to hear. I truly pray that your boyfriend will find saving faith in the Messiah Yeshua.

Have a look at our resources. Let me know how else I can be of help. If you welcome a telephone or Skype call, we can set an appointment.

Shalom and blessings,

Tuvya

At the end of this chapter you'll have an opportunity to do some analysis on my response to Danielle.

The same principles of being candid about the pitfalls of being unequally yoked apply to having sex outside of marriage. We should never affirm what Scripture prohibits, but we can choose meaningful words to speak the truth carefully and in love.

I've heard a couple of pastors share frankly, yet discreetly, about the negative impact of premarital sex on their own relationships and marriages. They got their point across without making accusations that would likely have brought the conversations to an end.

I'm not suggesting that you randomly bring up intimate details from your past! The point is, these pastors used their own mistakes as a nonjudgmental way to point out the problem of sin, while also building trust through their own transparency.

Don't Be a Spiritual Janitor

It isn't easy for Jewish-Gentile couples to come to pastors or Christian friends looking for spiritual guidance in their premarital situation. They aren't looking for someone to point out or try to clean up whatever messiness their relationship may entail. They need some positive advice and direction. You might have the best advice in the world without any platform to offer it.

A platform for communication is built on respect. Respect does not require us to affirm every choice people make. It also does not require us to convict them of their sin. That is the job of the Holy Spirit.

I remind myself that my purpose is not to fix them or clean up after them, but to create understanding.

Consider a couple I know who visited three different members of clergy before contacting Jews for Jesus. The Gentile partner is a Christian who is living with her Jewish boyfriend. First they met with the pastor of a cool, urban church who scolded them, pronouncing them "unequally yoked." His advice: break up!

I happen to know that pastor; he's close to the couple in age, he's well read, vibrant and enthusiastic in his faith—he had a lot to offer. But he began the conversation with a nonstarter. There was no place to go from there; the couple perceived his remarks as one more example of narrow-minded Christian rejection. They already felt alienated from synagogue life and now they were uncomfortable about going to the church.

Next, they went to the pastor of an older, mainline church in a nearby suburb. He told them about his own daughter who had converted to Judaism in order to marry her Jewish boyfriend. The pastor seemed satisfied with that. This totally deflated the Christian partner. She knew that converting to Judaism would require her to renounce Jesus, something she found unthinkable. Her Jewish boyfriend didn't think it was such a great option, either. While he did not share her beliefs, he recognized that many of the qualities that attracted him to her were inseparable from her faith.

The third person they visited was a rabbi of a progressive and hip synagogue. After listening to his explanation of Judaism for more than an hour, neither of them felt compelled to join his synagogue.

They went from one person who tried to convict them of sin and clean them up spiritually to another whose solution completely undermined one partner's identity and finally to someone whose ideas just didn't connect with them in any way. They were pretty discouraged by the time they came to me, but they weren't giving up.

And so, we three have been meeting to seek spiritual wisdom for their relationship. They understand that I fully subscribe to the Bible, including what says about relationships. And I'll admit, sometimes it is difficult to hold my own convictions without crawling up onto the seat of judgment. That's when I remind myself that my purpose is not to fix them or clean up after them, but to create understanding.

I hope to connect with couples in order to introduce them to a way out of their dilemma. I can't do that if I'm judging them and driving them away. I'm there to meet the couple where they are at, to create understanding between them, and to point them to the gospel. That's where they can find a common path to a mutually satisfying relationship with the living God. That also happens to be where they'll learn to trust His authority in their lives and in their relationship.

You can do everything you're supposed to do, yet not see the desired outcome.

When you have opportunities to meet with a couple like the one I described above, remember that the opportunity is what might be called "pre-evangelistic." You are meeting them at the point of need they have described. You can use the chart provided in chapter 4 to help them understand their challenges and remember your role as cross-cultural translator. When the challenge of religious differences comes up, there may be opportunities to share the gospel.

Success as God Measures It

Christians cannot presume upon God to change their partner's heart. Yet I have seen God pour out His grace to bring an unbelieving partner to faith. You can't know if God will or won't do that in any given situation; you can only be available for Him to use you.

One of the challenges of ministry is that you can do everything you're supposed to do, yet not see the desired outcome. Don't let that hinder you! Love and serve God faithfully, follow His lead in loving and serving others, and you'll experience success as God measures it. If you start with the premise that only the Holy Spirit can achieve a spiritual outcome in someone else's life, you won't become demotivated by situations like the one I'm about to describe:

Carrie was a strong evangelical Christian from Texas. She met her Jewish boyfriend, Aharon, while they were working for a social service outreach to children of single parents in an urban city center.

Aharon's father was from a very Orthodox Jewish family in New York. In fact, religion had been a point of contention within their family harmony even though both of his parents kept the Jewish religion.

We cannot predict or control outcomes. We can only do our best to create understanding.

Aharon loved Carrie. He was committed enough to marry her though he was pretty vocal about his dislike for her Christian faith.

Carrie loved Aharon. She hoped that her love would win him to faith in Jesus, and believed her faith was strong enough to endure his negative attitude toward Christianity until then. Meanwhile, in an effort to relate to him spiritually, she took an "Introduction to Judaism" class at a nearby Jewish community center.

However, the class in Judaism was raising questions for her. The rabbi said that Jews already had a relationship with God, so they didn't need "help" from any other religion. He also explained that Gentiles couldn't embrace Judaism unless they were willing to give up Jesus. "That's not going to happen," Carrie told everyone. She continued working hard to demonstrate her willingness to understand Aharon's religious world. On top of that, the class cost her lot of money.

Carrie called, asking if I could meet with the two of them. She wanted me to help explain her faith to Aharon in a way that he could understand from a Jewish cultural perspective. Aharon was willing to meet because he was trying to reciprocate Carrie's willingness to understand his faith.

I suggested six sessions to look into the Gospel of John, so Aharon could at least understand Carrie's faith. Then we could evaluate if there was anything further I could do to help. I explained, "Best of all, there is no charge."

Aharon showed up for each of the six lessons. He gained a new perspective and realized that what he had been taught about Jesus was not necessarily true. He heard and grasped the gospel message quite clearly, from a cultural context that he understood. That had been the purpose of the six meetings. And when they were over, he chose not to believe.

And yet, the "seed of the Word" has been planted. It's in the Lord's hands and Aharon's heart as to whether that seed will come to fruition. We cannot predict or control outcomes. We can only do our best to create understanding.

It's Complicated

Many of the dating couples I meet are reaching out because they are serious, often thinking towards marriage. At that point, they are still wading through their own cultural differences, when along come waves of expectations from their parents, siblings, relatives and friends of the family. The widening community of people and cultures voicing their views often comes as quite a surprise to the partners.

An Israeli guy in the San Fernando Valley, Gidi (short for Gideon), joined his family at their home every Friday evening for a cultural, but not especially religious Shabbat (Sabbath) dinner. He brought his "Christian girlfriend from Texas," as he usually called her.

Tracy told me that she couldn't understand Gidi's family at all. I thought she was overstating the cross-cultural nature of her experience at Gidi's home. I asked, "What didn't you understand about them?" "Everything they said to each other! They only speak 'Jewish' at home," she explained. Oy!

It hadn't occurred to Gidi that Tracy would feel isolated from him and his family because though they spoke to her in English, they only spoke Hebrew to one another. That's an extreme case, but it helps make the point: family and friends add even more cultural challenges to Jewish-Gentile couples.

Family and friends add even more cultural challenges to Jewish-Gentile couples.

Those challenges become even more pronounced when the couple decides to get married, and we'll discuss those challenges in the next chapter. But before we move on to that next relationship stage, I wanted to share an encouraging story from an encounter with a couple in the dating stage.

Melissa, a Jewish woman from a traditional background, contacted my office for a referral to a Messianic congregation that she and Luke (her Gentile Christian boyfriend) could attend. The three of us met together to see if we could better understand what was happening in their relationship.

She soon realized that a congregation wasn't the answer to her underlying question. She and Luke were looking for a way to find spiritual harmony. And while they were challenged by their different religious beliefs, Melissa found herself wanting to know more about Jesus. I asked her, "Can you tell the difference between your attraction to Luke and the draw in your heart toward Messiah Jesus?" She thought deeply before she answered. "I'm not sure that I know right now. But, even if my relationship with Luke doesn't work out, I have to know the truth about who Jesus is. I'm sure about that now."

It takes patience to walk alongside people, helping make discoveries like the one Melissa made. Sometimes the discovery will be heartbreaking, as in the case of "Jane" who was courageous enough to share what she learned from her experience, specifically to help others who might relate to her situation.

Letting Go of False Hope: Holding on to the Hope in Christ

by Jane

I was in college when I first met my Jewish boyfriend. At the time, my faith was not fully developed, nor was it mature enough to grasp the implications of being in a relationship with a Jewish man who did not share my belief in Jesus. However, even from the beginning I knew something was not right.

I sought counsel from my family and Christian friends. With time, I came to the decision that I should end things peacefully with him before our relationship got too serious. Despite my honest and heartfelt intentions, I could not let him go. His determination to make things work out made it even more complicated. Over the next four years of my college education I experienced brief moments of joy amidst years of emotional turmoil.

Though my boyfriend and I could agree on a lot of the Old Testament or Torah, we didn't see eye to eye on the New Testament. From his youth, David was taught that Jesus was a false prophet. In stark contrast, I grew up hearing and eventually came to believe that Jesus was the promised Messiah and the Son of God. It really became quite clear that Jesus was going to be the dividing issue that would undo our relationship.

While I tried to break up with David several times throughout college, I could never fully separate myself from him. I was simply in love and that was a strong feeling that I didn't want to lose. I was also living a fantasy that things would work out. I probably developed a false hope whenever he would attend Christian Bible studies or read the New Testament. He promised me that things would eventually work out. At one point, he said that he would not believe in something until he could believe it wholeheartedly. That gave me lingering hope that he might change.

It wasn't until after college that I decided that I had to end my relationship with David. I was just tired of trying to make things work out from my side alone. I gave up hope that he would honestly investigate the gospel or try to understand Jesus. I did not want to pressure David and he was not inclined to challenge or to sincerely change his faith.

What also made me decide to break things off was the fact that I never met David's family after four years of being with him. That pained me a great deal, because I understood that meant I could never be accepted or respected by them. David was actually living one life with me at school and another life with his family and community at home. I know that God could change David's heart, but it apparently was not going to be through my influence.

I do believe that breaking the relationship with my Jewish boyfriend was spiritually and emotionally the right choice for me. I was seriously spiritually tested during our relationship.

That in turn made me more passionate about pursuing God, reading my Bible and praying. It was hard to face that my spiritual growth was actually limited when I was with someone who simply did not support my beliefs nor encouraged them in my life.

As I look back on our relationship, I do not believe it was an accident that I met my ex-boyfriend and deeply cared for him. I believe that it is through the difficult moments and trials in life that a person can grow and mature the most. If life was perfect and nothing was challenging then I would be a shallow person. My faith would be weak and without any root.

I know that there is definite hope for Jewish and Gentile couples and that is through Yeshua (Jesus). Ironically, a relative of mine married a Messianic Jewish woman. Their life together is centered in common faith that Jesus is Lord, Savior and Messiah.

My heart goes out to Jewish-Gentile couples, because I know how hard it is when there is spiritual and emotional discord with one another. I want to encourage those who relate to my experience to stay strong in your faith and give your struggles and burdens to the Lord. I saw that I could not carry mine alone anymore, but Jesus could. He carried them for me, and for His chosen people, on the cross two thousand years ago.

Conclusion

I hope the stories you've just read paint a clear picture of some of the situations you are likely to encounter with Jewish-Gentile couples in their dating phase. In each situation you encounter, you'll need to determine where the ministry opportunities are: it might be primarily to a Christian who is uncertain about his or her involvement. It might be with a Jewish person who may or may not be open to hearing more about the Messiah. Or, if the couple is already quite committed to sharing their future, it will be to the pair of them, helping them to understand their challenges, and doing your best to offer the hope of spiritual harmony.

Exercise

Take another look at the letter to Danielle, the woman who reached out to me after her parents told her she had to choose between God and the Jewish man she is seeing.

The numbers on the next page represent the seven paragraphs of the letter, excluding the greeting and closing.

After each number, in one or two sentences, describe what you think each paragraph accomplishes.

HE SAID *then* SHE SAID

1. ____

____

____

2. ____

____

____

3. ____

____

____

4. ____

____

____

____

5. ____

____

____

____

6. ____

____

____

7. ____

____

____

Notice the order of the seven things you have just written. What bearing do you think that order has on the ability to connect with someone in Danielle's position?

Notice also that the letter combines "careful" words and phrases with very candid statements. What do you notice about the way they are balanced?

Would you see Jane's story as an appropriate resource to share with someone like Danielle? If not, why not, and if so, how would you present it?

Chapter 8
Married without Children

After a wedding, the duo is on the road to discovering their new identity as a family. They have blended two separate identities and disparate cultures. They need to choose which holidays to celebrate and how they will go about their celebrations. These considerations often require careful and sometimes painful discussions of what symbols and practices will be mutually acceptable.

Unresolved tensions that may have been overlooked while the couple was dating reappear. Some couples told me how, after the wedding, they began to realize that they would "have to compromise" about the identity, religion or training of their future children. Add into the discussion generational expectations coming from the extended family members and "wow." Guilt, shame and pressure on the couple to preserve ethnicity and/or religion became more acute. All that on top of the couples' newly married identity makes for some pretty complex and intense situations.

One couple told me about a quarrel they had over a simple birthday gift the wife had received. She unwrapped it, exclaimed with delight over a small figurine of an angel and promptly put it in the center of their dining room table. Her husband came home and, seeing the angel, exploded. She asked why he was angry but his response didn't make a lot of sense to her: "You're trying to bring Christianity into my house." To her it was an innocent little figurine. She never imagined he would see it as a Christian symbol being given a place of prominence in their home. He felt his deeply Jewish identity was being disregarded or even challenged.

This story perfectly illustrates how communication (or miscommunication, for that matter) involves many unspoken cultural signals. Cultural signals include artifacts, colors, pictures, hand gestures, numbers, facial expressions—all sorts of different cues send signals. In fact, I received a great tool that helped me become more aware of these cues during my cross-cultural communication studies. It's called, "12 Cultural Signal Systems." You'll see it at the end of this chapter.

I've heard so many stories about conflicts triggered by symbols, rituals, rites and life-cycle celebrations. These were often connected to holidays or family gatherings. Here are examples couples mentioned:

- Wedding ceremonies, receptions and anniversary celebrations
- Rites of passage, like Bar/Bat Mitzvahs, baptisms, birthdays and funerals
- Welcoming children: baby dedication, naming ceremony and circumcision
- Holidays: Passover, Easter, High Holy Days, Hanukkah and Christmas

Some of these bullet points will be elaborated upon as you continue working through this book. Depending on how actively you intend to pursue ministry to Jewish-Gentile couples, you may want to educate yourself further about these types of events.

Meanwhile, you can use the bullet points above as a list of suggested topics for a married-without-children couple to review so they can choose which are relevant for them to think through together. They might appreciate your presence as a "translator" for these discussions, or you may have already helped them develop the listening and questioning skills they need to feel comfortable having the discussions privately.

Many Jewish-Gentile partners also talked about the increased tension their differing religious beliefs pose at this stage in their relationship. After marriage, some couples begin to realize that hopes they may have cherished about their spouse's views might not be fulfilled.

Cultural signals include artifacts, colors, pictures, hand gestures, numbers, facial expressions— all sorts of different cues send signals.

An Open Door

The couple may begin asking themselves whether they can ever find what I've termed "spiritual harmony." The answer to that question will determine the depth of their spiritual intimacy for the rest of their lives. Remember that as the couple opens up about their hopes and fears, they also open a significant door for spiritual ministry.

For example, Virginia told me the exact moment that she was hard hit by the reality that she and Mike, her Jewish husband, were on different spiritual paths. She said, "I was lying in bed one night and was overcome with an awful fear that if Mike died, he wouldn't be with God." In fact, she was not only concerned that he wouldn't be with God, but that she, too, would be forever separated from Mike.

Mike loved Virginia, but he just didn't understand her fear. He had no spiritual or cultural basis for any particular belief about life after death. He'd been raised with a strong sense of Jewish ethics and concern for doing our part to make the world a better place while we're alive (remember *tikkun olam* from chapter 3). Like many Jewish people, he wasn't worried about what would happen after he died. He just wanted to do a good job of living life now.

Where could I begin the conversation? Respecting boundaries is key to building trust. That includes not barging into a sensitive subject a person has shown no interest in discussing. Mike certainly wasn't asking about eternal life. But since Virginia had brought up the subject, I could ask her (in his presence) why she was afraid that Mike "wouldn't be with God" after he died. That was a fair question under the circumstances, and it did not put pressure on Mike to speak about topics that were foreign to him.

As she looked at him, she told me that they have very different ideas about God. Mike added, "I believe in God, but not like she does. I believe God exists, but I just don't trust Him."

Jewish history is part of the collective consciousness of Jewish people and the past few hundred years have been pretty tough. There's the history of the Christian Crusades, the Catholic Church's Inquisition in Spain and intolerance toward Jews during the Reformation. Persecution of Jews in Czarist Russia or in Nazi Germany fortified Jewish mistrust of European Christians.

Of course evil people have done lots of awful things in the name of various good and noble causes. That's not grounds for distrusting God, but I wasn't there to question Mike's distrust. His participation in the conversation opened another door.

I wanted to test if Mike was open to discover something new about God. So I asked, "Since you believe He exists, what would you like God to do for you?" "Nothing actually," Mike responded. I told him, "Then it seems that prayer has already been answered."

It then became very natural for me to turn to Virginia and ask, "What do you want from God?" She answered from the depths of her being. "I want to know Him more. I want to see Him in my life. I want to know His plan and purpose for me. I just want to know Him better." Tears were streaming down her cheeks. I had no idea she would respond like this. I was simply giving her the same opportunity to express herself as I'd given Mike. Can you see the rhythm of going back and forth?

Mike looked a little embarrassed and puzzled. All this was foreign to him. I translated the experience, "That's what trusting God looks like." It turned into a significant moment for Mike and for Virginia. Who knew that God was going to open up that door? It was an opportunity for cross-cultural translation, creating new understanding and a connection for them.

Trust is a choice. Perhaps in that moment, Mike caught a glimpse of the kind of trust in God he might one day wish to have.

The Family Factor

Learning how to build a marriage that takes cultural and religious differences into account would be complicated enough if it only involved the couple, but what would a marriage be without in-laws? Family gatherings bring a whole new set of challenges—especially if those gatherings are for the holidays.

Eric didn't realize that when he brought his new wife, Sandy, to his parents' home for Passover. Sandy, a Gentile born-again follower of Jesus, looked forward to getting to know her Jewish in-laws. She knew about Passover from the Bible and was excited to celebrate it with her new family. Thankfully, everyone was speaking English . . . but all at the same time and very loudly!

Sandy was overwhelmed by the apparent discord. Her family just didn't speak to one another like that. She soon realized they were not angry at each other, but she was too intimidated to join the conversation. She didn't know where to jump in or even whether her participation would be welcome. As Sandy described her experience, she echoed many who described feeling like an outsider or someone who was not a "member of the tribe."

How weird to find jarring cross-cultural differences within your own family and to experience culture shock in the home of your relatives. Eric wasn't insensitive, like Gidi had been. He was simply unaware of how different his family was from Sandy's, or how that would make her feel.

Eric, in turn, described his discomfort at being expected to participate in non-Jewish traditional family practices at the home of his in-laws. He mentioned prayer before meals. Family members on either side would take his hands, close their eyes and Sandy's father would pray. Eric didn't know what to do at that point. The first time it happened, no one told him what it all meant. Eric experienced the same sort of culture shock that Sandy had described from being in his parents' home.

The best approach is direct and casual, leading to a friendly time of discovery.

When couples don't live in close proximity to one another's families they might not experience scenarios like these until just before the wedding—even after in some cases. If you are ministering to couples who are dating or very newly married and haven't yet visited the homes of relatives for the first time, you can help by encouraging the couple to describe what is typical for their family's meals and holiday celebrations. Ask them to try to imagine it from the perspective of a person who is likely to find it all very new, and to help their partner know how to fit in.

When Mom and Dad Ask for Help

Parents of Jewish-Gentile couples frequently ask for advice about how to relate with sensitivity to a Jewish son or daughter-in-law. Family members often want someone to serve as a sort of cross-cultural bridge so they can explore the world of their new family member.

What can you say when a parent says, "My Jewish daughter-in-law is coming to our house for Thanksgiving. What should I serve?" I suggest they begin by asking their new daughter-in-law whether she has any dietary restrictions, or what she likes to eat. If that's too awkward, they can ask their son if he knows of any dietary restrictions. The best approach is direct and casual, leading to a friendly time of discovery.

Answering questions is one way you can give support to parents of JGCs. But what about a parent who asks if you'll meet with his son or daughter and his/her spouse? Let me tell you how I responded to one such request.

It all started with an email. "Dad" was an evangelical Christian living on the East Coast. His daughter had married a young Jewish professional and they were living in California. Dad told me how much he cared for both the "kids," and of his growing concern for them.

They had been married for two years. The son-in-law had attended a family celebration around Christmas, but he seemed uncomfortable and uninvolved. The daughter had told Dad that they seemed to be settling down in "two separate lives" in the same household. The father wondered if I could meet with the couple.

My initial ministry was to the father. I explained the cross-cultural nature of his daughter's marriage. Dad of course had his own concerns for his son-in-law's spiritual well being, and for the happiness of his daughter. I explained that his daughter was sorting out her own identity, including her relationship with the Lord, in the context of her new household. She needed to know that Dad loved and accepted her as she struggled to figure things out.

We can't be spiritual hammers to wear down or pound the gospel into a Jewish partner.

I also told him I'd be glad to meet with the couple, but on the condition that they would know ahead of time that I'm a Messianic Jew who specializes in work with Jewish-Gentile couples. Some parents have asked if they can introduce me as a "Jewish educator," a non-specific "minister" or even a "rabbi." Lack of candor could seriously damage a couple's trust in a parent who refers them to me, and would also start any relationship we might build on the wrong foot.

I frequently tell the Christian parents or partners in a Jewish-Gentile couple, "I can't be a spiritual hammer to wear down or pound the gospel into a Jewish partner." What I can do, and you can, too, is try to help those parents appreciate the Jewish cultural sensitivities of their new or soon-to-be family member. If you are not Jewish, reading this book will clue you in to some of those sensitivities, but you don't have to be immersed in a particular culture to help someone be sensitive to that culture. The main thing they need to know is that many things that seem obvious or normal to them will be quite out of the ordinary to someone from a different culture. They should make people feel welcome to participate in family rituals, but not assume that these rituals will be understood or embraced.

For example, whenever our children bring guests into our home to share a meal, I pause before we eat. Those guests might not share our faith in Messiah Jesus so I make a point of telling them what I'm about to do. "I want to thank God, because that's what we do as a family at meal times. But, I don't want to impose our faith on you. You are welcome to take part in our time of thanking

God . . . or not. There's no requirement to join in." Surprisingly, that usually works well to set guests at ease. They feel welcome and not pressured.

Speaking of children, we have been considering the spiritual challenges that a couple without children might face. The anticipation or birth of a child brings with it a whole new set of challenges, which we'll address in the next chapter. But first . . .

A Valuable Tool

On the next page, you'll see the categories for twelve cultural signals that people use to express themselves, with bullet points giving examples of each category. I received it from my mentor, Dr. Donald K. Smith, during his cross-cultural communication course at Western Seminary. This tool helped me study and understand elements of other peoples' cultures and I hope you'll find it helpful too. In this case, most of the examples are taken from Jewish culture.

You can copy it to help couples ask one another about the meanings of whichever cultural symbols they don't understand (or even to help you understand more about symbols you may be curious about from this list).

Conclusion

Because there is more at stake in the relationship after marriage, challenges and tensions are all the more difficult. If you haven't used the chart in chapter 4 before now, remember it is a great tool for making conversations more objective and less likely to become a "blame game." The 12 Cultural Signal Systems serves the same purpose. Seeing elements of culture listed in a document someone else crafted enables couples to discuss sensitive matters with a bit of detachment and objectivity. That reduces the sense of threat and gives people opportunities to describe what these things mean to them.

Exercise

1. Reread the third paragraph of this chapter, about the couple and the angel figurine. Then go to page 33, locate the "Together without Children" stage and read that stage all the way across the chart. Answer the following:

   a. Which cultural categories came into play for the couple in this story?

   b. If you were meeting with that couple and the wife told you this story, what questions would you ask each of them to help create understanding about what happened?

2. See how many more bullet points you can fill in on the 12 Cultural Signal Systems to express your own culture. (Use p. 78 to list them.) Can you see how these cultural expressions might signal something very different to people from a different culture than yours?

12 Cultural Signal Systems

Verbal speech
- terminology (language: Hebrew or technical: Tenach)
- prayers
- expressions "messianic" v. "Christian"
- exclamations: "Oy" "Shalom" "Amen"
- names of the Lord: G-d, L-rd, Jesus, Yeshua or "Yeshu" (rabbinic rebuff)

Written
- Hebrew
- Bible
- Jewish or Christian authors and themes
- prayer book, hymnal, Haggadah

Numerical
- Hebrew numbering, 18 for blessing or luck
- 7th day, month or year
- numbering of Bible verses

Pictorial
- Jewish art (e.g., Marc Chagall)
- family pictures
- scenes from Israel or Holocaust pictures
- the cross or a Star of David (Magen David)

Artifacts
- degel Israeli (Flag for the State of Israel)
- Kippot (head covering, male)
- hanukkiah (Hanukkah candelabra)
- menorah
- Shabbat candles or a wedding unity candle
- shofar (ram's horn)
- Kiddish cup or communion cup
- matzah or communion wafers

Audio
- traditional songs
- chanted prayers
- shofar (ram's horn) sounds for Rosh Hashanah
- ring tones

Kinesics
- motions or gestures (e.g., Israeli motion for "just a second")
- davening (bowing) motions in Jewish prayer
- waving Lulav on Sukkot
- ceremonial candle lighting
- mother smother hugs
- way of touching (e.g., blessing to pray over children or consecrate someone)
- baptism or mikvah

Optical
- blue and white colors and lights
- red and green lights or colors
- olive skin
- Hanukkah or Shabbat lights

Tactile
- matzah
- old hands
- fringes on a prayer shawl (tsit-tsit)
- hummus (food)
- religious clothing

Spatial
- places of worship or prayer
- baptism or mikvah pool
- Passover table
- personal spatial distance

Temporal
- calendar
- Shabbat, 7th day
- Holy Days and festivals

Olfactory
- foods
- spices for services or besamim/havdallah service at end of Sabbath

Chapter 9
Married with Children

Sharon was raised in a Catholic Christian home in Iowa and Norman was from a traditional Jewish home in western Tennessee. They married and made a home together in Des Moines. About two years later their son, Samuel, was born. They were devoted parents and both wanted to be sure he had a meaningful spiritual education.

Though she hadn't converted to Judaism, Sharon regularly took part in their synagogue and was committed to the family's participation in Judaism and Jewish community life. After Samuel's eighth birthday, Sharon discovered that she and her husband had very different visions for his ongoing religious training.

Samuel had been receiving religious instruction in Judaism and would soon begin bar mitzvah preparation. And with bar mitzvah lessons in view, Sharon realized that it was important to her that Samuel would also learn about Jesus, since He is the Messiah of the Jewish people, too.

She asked their rabbi if he would include some instruction about Jesus the Messiah as part of the synagogue education program. His answer was an emphatic "absolutely not!" Perplexed, Sharon contacted our Jews for Jesus office for some help or resources.

After living with her Jewish husband for almost a decade, and despite her occasional involvement with the synagogue, Sharon remained unschooled about some basic facts of Jewish life and culture. That was apparent right away by her request for a (non-Messianic) rabbi to teach her son about the Messiah Jesus.

During our initial emails Sharon told me that she and Norman were visiting his parents in California. They were staying less than a mile from a church where I would be speaking just two days later. We quickly made arrangements and Sharon gave me the address of a convenient location for us to meet.

When I arrived, I was surprised to find myself at a Jewish assisted living facility where, as it turned out, Norman's parents were residents. I was a little nervous about having a culturally sensitive conversation in the coffee shop of the residential hall, but I wasn't as nervous as Norman turned out to be. He'd shown up for Sharon's sake, but it was clearly her concern that was driving the conversation.

Sharon reiterated her disappointment that their rabbi had refused to teach their son about Jesus and asked if I could help with that part of Samuel's education. I suggested that this conversation should probably take place between her and Norman—not with me. Norman seemed relieved and was quite in agreement. We left that part of the plan for them to manage in private, and they could let me know in the future if they both wanted me to participate.

Sharon still had other questions. She didn't understand what she saw as a traditional Jewish resistance to Jesus and the gospel. Norman was still uncomfortable, yet interested in this phase of the conversation.

Sharon "complained" to me that Norman was barely Jewish because he didn't believe in a Messiah.

It was left to me to explain how so many terrible things have been done in the name of Jesus throughout history. We could agree that Jesus never sanctioned any of those atrocities, but that it was understandable that Jewish people who had suffered at the hands of those claiming loyalty to Him were, at the very least, wary of Christians, and in many cases, of Christ.

Then I explained to Sharon how Jews in America traditionally did not make a clear distinction between the terms "Gentile" and "Christian." Therefore, Hitler's Germany was viewed as a "Christian" nation. Jewish people got the message that the gospel was bad news for Jews.

Sharon was amazed, and her new understanding of her husband's feelings showed. Norman began to relax and warm up. It turned out that his Tennessee upbringing had exposed him to lots of Bible Belt Christians. He shared that they were well meaning, but had been insensitive to his Jewish perspective. I understood that. We were able to continue the discussion with some ease.

After a while, the subject of Samuel's religious education resurfaced. While Sharon was no longer asking me for help without her husband's permission, she reiterated that she wanted their son to learn about the Messiah Jesus, since that was an important part of her Christian faith.

To support her case, Sharon "complained" to me that Norman was barely Jewish because he didn't believe in a Messiah. In his defense Norman said, "There are many messiahs (or people claiming to be), so how can we know for sure which is the right one?" By the way, this is not an uncommon argument.

I asked him how he knew this idea—that we can't verify any one person as the real Messiah—was true. He said this was what his rabbi had taught in the synagogue when he was growing up. I suggested that there might be another answer found in the Scriptures, if he was willing to look.

I offered to send literature that would shed some light on what the Bible teaches about the long expected Jewish Messiah. Both partners said they'd be glad to obtain any such resources that are available through Jews for Jesus.

Beneath the Dreams

Now you see what couples meant when they said that discord over how to raise children is a huge challenge.

Many couples told me how they'd talked about their dreams for future children while they were dating, or even during premarital counseling. But remember, there are some unknown realities beneath those dreams. Couples can't always see some of the deeper core identity issues that will surface after they are married.

I saw how a lot of dreamy discussions and earnest promises did not work out as expected once real children entered a family. Couples' deeply held cultural expectations concerning the identity of those children were often out of sync, prompting them to seek counsel from parents and others.

Couples can't always see some of the deeper core identity issues that will surface after they are married.

The couple's parents, of course, will have their own deeply held cultural expectations concerning the identity of their grandchildren. Parents and extended family can create an atmosphere of competition over the identity of the children.

Often the sticking points were, "I want my kids/grandkids to be Jews" and "My children/grandchildren should know the Savior Jesus, like I do." Some people chose to ignore this discussion before they got married or pregnant, because their relationship was "so perfect" otherwise. They just didn't want to "rock the boat." Then, when the babies came along, subsequent discussions rocked the boat pretty hard.

Jewish-Gentile parents I surveyed described two main challenges in this season of their lives. First, they wondered, "What is our child's identity?" And second, "Who and how will we teach them to integrate our different heritages and values?" Mom and Dad might have very different ideas about the answers to these questions . . . and children can get mixed signals.

At the beginning of this book I talked about the process of children learning their culture, that is, *enculturation*. The process happens naturally, but becomes tense when dealing with a blend of different sets of cultural "software." It is crucial for the marriage that parents discuss candidly the cultural values that really matter to them.

Naturally, it's better to have that conversation before children are present. If parents don't come up with a thoughtful strategy of how to communicate culture to their children, it will happen in a less-than-thoughtful way. And, if the parents have unresolved cross-cultural conflicts, those conflicts will be become part of the enculturation process. That can produce some unintended consequences.

For example, I was interviewing Mary, a mom from an Irish Catholic background. Her husband,

Judah, was a secular Jew. This couple had been unable to resolve how to communicate their family identity to their children, or even how to discuss a family "religion." So they didn't. They were happy enough for their children to decide those things for themselves when they grew up.[1]

These were both bright professional people who possessed enormous personal warmth and humor. I enjoyed hearing them tease one another about their starkly different cultures. I wondered how their daughter, who was raised in such an open, self-aware and culturally mixed home would sort out her own identity. I tried to remain expressionless when their 17-year-old daughter passed through the room dressed in gothic black, covered with piercings and tattoos. Her mom told me their daughter was a devotee of Wicca.

What can we do?

We can help Jewish-Gentile couples explore possible strategies of religious cultural training and ethnic identity formation for their children. We can extend support, perspective and wisdom to couples and parents as they struggle to grapple with the challenges of enculturation for their children.

Perhaps our most important ministry would be to help children connect with their ethnic Jewish heritage while finding eternal life in Messiah Jesus, just as Sharon had hoped. But that won't happen if one parent invites participation while the other disapproves.

Chances are they will both appreciate your help in suggesting a thoughtful way to proceed.

Creating trust, building on that trust and maintaining it are all crucial in our ability to extend spiritual ministry to Jewish-Gentile couples and their children. Realizing what is happening with their relationships without judging them helps to lay the foundation for that trust. Beyond that, we have to continue doing things to preserve that trust. This is the gateway to extending spiritual ministry to the Jewish-Gentile couples and their families.

If you are invited to continue meeting with a couple, I advocate a holistic approach that embraces Jewish-Gentile couples and their children—and one in which you take advantage of all the resources that are available to help you serve the couple. This includes the specialized materials that Jews for Jesus offers to show why we believe Jesus is the Jewish Messiah, but it can also be a ministry for the whole church. (See chapter 10.)

The partners may or may not agree to include you in advising them or participating with them in the process of helping with cross-cultural religious instruction for their kids. Either way, chances are they will both appreciate your help in suggesting a thoughtful way to proceed. You can begin to do that by familiarizing yourself with the following.

Strategies for Enculturating Children of Jewish-Gentile Couples

While doing my own research, I met M. A. Callahan, a graduate student at USC who was doing similar research. She identified these four enculturation strategies:

1. Team Leadership
2. Delegated Leadership
3. Secular Leadership
4. Families without Clear Leadership

It can be helpful for you to bring up these four different ways of passing on culture to children, so that couples can identify where they are or would like to be in this process.

Team Leadership: husband and wife are equally committed to the religious training of their children and collaborate as active partners. Together they discuss and decide which religion is going to be provided for the child or whether a combination of both will be presented.

Delegated Leadership: one parent is primarily responsible for the religious training of the child. This can happen by default or by agreement between the parents. In the research sample that I interviewed, it was most often the wife in a Jewish-Gentile couple who bore the responsibility of delegated leadership.

Secular Leadership: the couple chooses to present a secular path for their children. This path might be chosen to avoid potential cross-cultural religious conflict or simply because a secular outlook was preferred. If the former, the possibility remained for children to form their own identity by observing and acquiring cultural beliefs from one or both of their parents.

Families without Clear Leadership: unlike the first three, this is not really a strategy but the clear lack of one. It is often the result of ambivalence or ambiguity in the religious identities of the parents. As they struggle to sort out their own cultural identities, they inadvertently become conveyers of cultural confusion. This is different from a chosen neutrality or secular outlook. In this situation, children are not given tools for analyzing culture. They lack parental guidance to help them form ethnic identity or an awareness of the elements of cultures that express religious beliefs.

Most of the Jewish-Gentile couples I interviewed, especially those who had children, believed that children need a clear cultural foundation to help them form an ethnic identity and express their religious beliefs. But resources to do this are limited in their perspective. Psychologists, sociologists, marriage and family counselors and clergy have written books for coping with dual identity or blended religious family life. Unfortunately, none that I have found is written from an evangelical perspective that appreciates Jewish culture in a mixed-marriage setting.

You may be asked by a Christian wife, as I have been, "In what practical ways can I bring harmony to our home if my husband cannot accept Jesus as Messiah and I feel the need to talk to our children about it?"

My response to that question:
Speaking with your husband about Jesus and sharing spiritual subjects with your children are two separate matters. Your relationship with your husband is based on an intimacy that you share with no one else. You and he must work to build/preserve intimacy in your marriage. That should include a commitment to mutual respect for one another's beliefs.

You have to know what you believe and why, and be willing to hear what he believes and why. Ask for the same opportunity that you would grant your spouse to share your beliefs and your heart for Jesus. The next step will be to trust the Lord to open his understanding. Your duty is to love your husband. Trust the Lord to move within him according to the ways of His Holy Spirit.

Your children are a shared responsibility. Their spiritual training is a loving duty that you share. Talk it through with your husband and find agreement about how to proceed. Your hope is that one day you all will share saving faith in the Messiah Jesus.

Conclusion
Couples choose either to teach their children about two religions, one faith or none. We can come alongside them and encourage the hope of preserving Jewish identity on one hand, and finding a mutual faith to pass on at the same time. The best outcome is if both partners will be open to seeing how this is possible through a relationship with the one living God through His Son, Jesus. After all, His Jewish identity is undisputed in Scripture and His love and reconciling power is for people of all ethnicities.

Exercise

Part One

Find the following phrases in the story and answer the questions.

1. Norman seemed relieved

What, specifically, was Norman's relief in response to?

What general principle can you draw from this?

2. Norman was still uncomfortable, yet interested in this phase of the conversation.

What topic of conversation caused Norman to be both uncomfortable and interested?

What does the combination of discomfort and interest tell you about Norman?

3. Norman began to relax and warm up

What caused Norman to relax and warm up?

How did Norman's relaxing change the course of the conversation?

4. To support her case, Sharon "complained" to me that Norman was barely Jewish because he didn't believe in a Messiah.

What knowledge do you now have about Jewish identity that would give Sharon a more realistic perspective?

If you were participating in this conversation, how might you address her mistaken idea in a way that would not make her feel that you were taking sides?

5. In his own defense, Norman said, "There are many messiahs (or people claiming to be), so how can we know for sure which is the right one?"

There was a two part response to Norman's statement. What were the two parts?

Part Two

1. When Sharon reached out for help, what did she hope the outcome of this first meeting would be?

2. What was the actual outcome of the first meeting?

3. Do you think Sharon was disappointed? Why or why not?

4. What principles can you draw from this about first meetings with Jewish-Gentile couples?

1. Of course, all children must decide for themselves what they believe and how to live when they grow up regardless of their enculturation. That doesn't mean that their parents should not communicate their own beliefs and values to them when they are young.

Chapter 10
Partnering with Your Local Congregation

If you have JGC neighbors, you should feel free to invite them to your local church or Messianic congregation. Note: most of the material in this chapter applies to predominantly Gentile churches unaccustomed to Jewish visitors. If you lead or attend a Messianic congregation, you might skip to the next chapter.

You might want to wait for a special event (maybe a concert or special speaker) that you have reason to believe they would enjoy or find especially interesting. If they have children, invite the family to a holiday event, or see if the parents are interested in sending the kids to daily vacation Bible school.

An invitation for a specific event gives people more reason to accept than a simple invitation to come to a regular worship service "sometime." Just make sure that both partners understand what will take place at the event so they can both be comfortable, or at least prepared. Special events can give the couple snapshots of what your local church or Messianic congregation has to offer.

If the couple has shown an interest in knowing what the Bible teaches, invite them to a Bible study. Make sure that other participants know beforehand that they should not expect the Jewish partner to be the resident Old Testament "scholar." This can be embarrassing if, as is often true, they don't know the Bible very well. And, if the Jewish partner has been to religious school, she or he might share a rabbinic story or perspective that is not consistent with your faith or Bible teaching. Traditional Jewish teachings can be highly interesting and speculative, but somewhat confusing if non-Jewish participants aren't aware of the nature of rabbinic teachings.

Attend the Bible study with the JGC. You may need to provide some cross-cultural translation. Spend time with them after the study, maybe over coffee, to find out their impressions, what they found interesting, where they agreed, disagreed or were curious to know more.

The Big Picture: Is Your Church Culturally Aware and Prepared?

Jewish-Gentile couples told me they often felt marginalized in both church and synagogue experiences.

To be fair, wherever they go, one partner is always going to feel like more of an "outsider" than the other. Their ability to feel at home in a new community just might depend on their own cultural flexibility. But your congregation can also help put them at ease.

The best ministry happens when Christians work together to reach others with the love of Messiah, helping one another to make disciples. That's why I advocate that churches, especially those in areas with a significant number of Jewish-Gentile couples, become partners in ministry to Jewish-Gentile couples and their families.

I suggest a holistic approach. Don't assume that welcoming Jewish-Gentile couples into your church is just another task for the pastor. It is crucial to have the understanding, participation and blessing of the leadership team, who can help the rest of the congregation set the tone for an acceptance of cultural diversity.

The whole church should be encouraged and prepared to embrace Jewish-Gentile couples and their children. That means being able to appreciate people who are different ethnically and culturally. That is what the body of Messiah is meant to be . . . many diverse disciples of Jesus, united in helping others to know and become His disciples. Some congregations are more naturally inclined to understand and appreciate diversity; others need encouragement.

> *Don't assume that welcoming Jewish-Gentile couples into your church is just another task for the pastor.*

If your congregation needs encouragement, remind fellow members that Jewish context and culture are seen throughout the whole Bible. Exploring and embracing the Jewish underpinnings of the Christian faith will not only help Jewish visitors feel at home, it will deepen the church's own understanding of God's plan of salvation.

Remember too, a Jewish presence in your congregation creates a whole new set of educational, historical and spiritual interests—providing an enriching cross-cultural experience. There is mutual blessing for Jews and Gentiles in a congregation where ethnic diversity is appreciated and spiritual unity in the Messiah is valued.

Church Champions

If you have a vision for this to happen in your church, you might be the "champion," the activist to help bring it about. Champions serve as the point people to carry the vision for a particular ministry, in this case, Jewish-Gentile couples ministry, so that others can understand and participate. Just as churches need champions who advocate for children's ministries, or for global missions, they also need champions to open up congregations for ministry to Jewish-Gentile couples.

If you are the pastor or part of the church leadership staff, I encourage you to use this book to train a few other champions and work as a team. If you are not part of the church's leadership team, you'll want to talk to the right people about your vision. One person can make a big difference in a church, but it needs to be a team effort.

Champions advocate steps to welcome JGCs. They often seek ongoing training and partnerships with more experienced workers who can assist them. They take on the primary responsibility for Jewish-Gentile couple ministry in their community.

Champions serve as the point people to carry the vision for a particular ministry.

Champions can also address doubts or concerns that others might raise. Here's one doubt I hope you won't hear in your church, but you should be prepared to address. What if someone says, "I respect my Jewish friends too much to tell them they need Jesus. They are very ethical people, and besides, doesn't the Bible teach that they have their own covenant with God?"

If a person or group of people in your church isn't sure that the gospel of Messiah Jesus is the only hope of salvation for Jewish people, just like it is for Gentiles, then it is absolutely of first order to settle that point. If Jesus and all of His first followers were Jewish, how is it disrespectful to want to introduce Jewish friends to Him?

Even more, if the Bible teaches that all people need Jesus, who are we to disagree? If Jesus isn't the Savior for all, then He isn't the Savior at all. And, if first century Messianic Jews had not reached out to non-Jews, the church would not be here today. They were willing to be misunderstood and sometimes rejected that others might be saved, and we need to be willing to take similar risks. That's what you do when you love people.

Be prepared to point out biblical passages such as,

> Jesus said to him, "I am the way, the truth, and the life. No one comes to the Father except through Me. (John 14:6)
>
> Nor is there salvation in any other. For there is no other name under heaven given among men by which we must be saved. (Acts 4:12)
>
> For I am not ashamed of the gospel of Christ, for it is the power of God to salvation for everyone who believes, for the Jew first and also for the Greek [gentile]. (Romans 1:16)

Church members are not all equally gifted when it comes to evangelism, but all should be able to encourage and pray for those who are actively involved in reaching out to unbelievers, whether Jewish or Gentile.

Extending a Welcome

Jewish-Gentile couples might remain "invisible" until you make a point of welcoming them and showing that they are not an oddity or social "outliers." Jewish people are a subculture in North America. Most will not take it for granted that they will be welcomed and affirmed as Jews among a non-Jewish majority. People are sensitive to signs and signals to let them know where they stand.

One person can make a big difference in a church, but it needs to be a team effort.

Sometimes it just takes a brief statement like, "Jewish-Gentile couples are welcome here" on your church website or in a local newspaper ad that advertises your services and special events. Sound too simple? You might be surprised to find out how much such a small effort is appreciated. In a sermon or Bible study about biblical Israelites, if the pastor or teacher is aware of Jewish visitors, a welcoming word about how glad they are that some "descendants of the people from the narrative we are studying are with us in our church today." A hearty "Shalom" as the pastor greets the congregation is a good way to let Jewish people know they are welcome—and hopefully others will enjoy that bit of Jewish culture.

Another way of letting Jewish people know they are welcome is to understand sensitivities and what is likely to be off-putting. Phrases such as "the Jews" might be used by Jewish people but sound pejorative coming from others. Also, hearing Scripture readings that speak of "the Jews" seeking to kill Jesus might confirm a person's worst fears that the New Testament and the church are anti-Jewish. I'm not suggesting you skip over such Scripture verses! But a brief side note after such a reading can easily relieve that fear. (E.g., "By the way, the term 'the Jews' in verse __ does not refer to all Jewish people. Remember that Jesus was Jewish, and so were all His first followers, including most if not all the writers of the gospels. The Jews referenced here were a group of religious leaders.")

A Jewish friend called me after hearing a sermon involving the Pharisees. The pastor, for all his skill in biblical exposition, had not imagined that someone would identify with the Jewish leaders that he had vilified without providing adequate context or cultural background. I needed to explain the context and assure my friend that the pastor was no anti-Semite.

Responding to Jewish Visitors

Jewish-Gentile couples might attend your local congregation, ministry, small groups or classes for any number of reasons. Some might come out of curiosity. A Jewish partner might attend as a "favor" to their Christian partner, or simply to show that they are open-minded. Sometimes the Jewish partner will accompany a Christian as a gesture of conciliation when religious faith has been a point of contention. If the couple has children, they might want to see if your community is "Jewish-friendly" and has anything to offer them as a family.

I suggest that you do not presume on the motivation of either partner. If you are aware of JGC visitors, greet them as you would anyone else. How can I put this? Just be "cool" and trust that the Lord is at work in their lives if they are making the effort to be with you. Make them feel welcome, like anyone else.

While it's good to cultivate an appreciation for Jewish people in your congregation, help people to understand it won't be helpful to go overboard in expressing that appreciation. Showing respect and interest in a person's Jewish background is affirming—but too much enthusiasm over a person's Jewishness can be scary.

How will you know if a Jewish-Gentile couple is visiting your church? If the last name is Cohen or Rosen, you can be pretty sure you have a Jewish guest. But it doesn't work the other way around; not all Jewish people have traditionally Jewish-sounding names. For example, you wouldn't know from the name "Scarlett Johansson" that the screen actress grew up in New York with an Ashkenazi (East European) Jewish mother.

It's always a good idea to greet any visitor or visiting couple by saying you're glad they came. Ask if they live in the area and how they happened to find out about your church. If they saw your welcome to Jewish-Gentile couples on the website or newspaper ad, they may mention it at that point—or not.

If you have a lot of Jewish friends, you may have a sense that a visitor is Jewish, but be sensitive in how you confirm your supposition. For example, don't ask, "Excuse me, but are you a Jew?" Some of us have experienced anti-Semitism from people who asked that very question. My first reaction is to answer, "Why do you want to know?"

So, how do you find out that point of information without putting a Jewish person on the spot? It's actually pretty easy. Simply ask, "Excuse me for asking, but are you a Gentile?" A Jewish person isn't going to be offended. They would just say no and might even find the question humorous. (We don't hear that one very often.) Your sensitivity to their feelings might even be a point for engaging in conversation. By the way, if the person responds, "What's a Gentile?" it is a pretty sure sign that they are one!

Showing respect and interest in a person's Jewish background is affirming—but too much enthusiasm over a person's Jewishness can be scary.

Small Groups

Does your church have small groups? If so, as more JGCs attend, create at least one small group that deals with cross-cultural issues and, if there are enough couples, have Jewish-Gentile couples' challenges as the focus of one such group. This could be a unique and welcoming feature.

Small groups are appealing and helpful for couples seeking community, especially a community where their distinct situation is understood, if not common to others in the group. Maybe you don't live in an especially Jewish area, but you have one JGC that's interested in a small group that meets their unique needs; you might see about recruiting other couples where one partner is a Christian and the other isn't to share a small group. While the cultures will differ, the fact that they can meet other couples who also deal with religious tensions could still be helpful.

A small group can be especially appropriate for Jewish partners if they are already familiar with the social structure known as the Havurah. Havurot (plural) are Jewish community groups that are a part of contemporary American Jewish life. They are a perfect setting for exploring the cross-cultural struggles of Jewish-Gentile couples and for sharing the often quite humorous cultural gaffs that all experience. Typically the Havurah has a facilitator to encourage discussion and who ensures that the environment is safe, non-judgmental and where all voices are heard. It is a shared learning experience where everyone is expected to contribute. (More about this in chapter 11.)

Mixed couples that include non-believers or seekers will likely be attracted to a congregation where they are accepted and included, especially if it offers the more intimate community setting of a small group.

While Jewish people might look like ordinary American "white people," we aren't.

Just remember, unbelieving partners, whether Jewish or Gentile, can't be expected to understand the terminology or rituals of a Christian community. Their starting vocabulary is going to be different. Remember your cross-cultural-translator mode to help create understanding. They want to be included, but not given condescending explanations. If you are leading a small group of mixed couples, you can ask people to list any religious words or rituals they don't understand.

What Will Happen?
What are some implications of ministry to Jewish-Gentile couples in your church?

If you are successful in showing JGCs that your congregation is a good place for them to seek spiritual harmony, more Jewish-Gentile couples and their children might show up as word spreads. The best of what could happen is that you will see Jews and Gentiles coming to saving faith in Jesus!

Remember that an increase in the number of Jewish people in your congregation will affect your culture. If you are part of a community that has only one noticeable cultural "flavor," help make others aware that you will need to make room for more. Church communities that have a hard time seeing beyond their own majority culture sometimes find it difficult to welcome strangers.

While Jewish people might look like ordinary American "white people," we aren't. Historically we have been a minority everywhere we have lived except in the Jewish homeland. We have been outsiders who became insiders while continuing to be at least bicultural. When we feel at home, you'll know it because our Jewish culture will become more obvious—often expressed in questions or comments about things that are culturally foreign to us.

How can your church respond? Just keep the Bible and the gospel as your core, while remaining flexible enough to try new ways of being a congregation of Jesus-followers—perhaps even with a little more Jewish flavor. For a small example, since communion was originally part of a Jewish Passover, you might have people asking to change the bread or wafers that your church uses to matzah.

Change and adaptation, challenging as they may be, can produce new life and growth.

You might be surprised at the variety of responses a change like that can bring . . . some will love it, others will struggle with any change from what is familiar. Within institutions, whatever is outside the norm can be perceived as a threat. That's why it's important for local congregations to remember change and adaptation, challenging as they may be, can produce new life and growth.

I think back to the 1970s, when God was working among the counterculture community. College and post-college-age young people were going through a dramatic culture change typified by long hair, psychedelic culture depicted in art and distinctive clothing, sexual promiscuity, tension with all authority and drug use. And yet, God worked within that community.

Many churches at the time discovered the discomfort of culture change. They had to decide if they could embrace those young counterculture people who were so extremely outside of their social norm. The body of Christ grew dramatically where churches were able to embrace the counterculture messiness—and partner with God in patiently helping people become disciples. A lot of those not-so-young-anymore people are now highly effective church and mission leaders within the American Christian community—thanks to the patience and willingness of mature believers to see beyond cultural norms.

I'm reminded of the wisdom and research of missiologist Paul Pierson, who taught that spiritual awakenings and renewal movements always begin on the margins of a society. By definition, that is where Jewish-Gentile couples see themselves. We ought to anticipate that the Lord is preparing a spiritual harvest among those people who see themselves on the margins of our communities.

Specialized Resources for Jewish-Gentile Couples

Churches or Messianic congregations can add value to their Jewish-Gentile ministry by offering seminars, studies and events that are seasonal and relevant. Participants might suggest topics or events or choose from a prepared list. Scheduling these seminars should take into account the needs of families with children. Weekly classes or seminars for adults running in tandem with a children's program could offer a great ministry for the whole family.

Conclusion

Ministry is meant to be a team effort, so partnering with local congregations is an important factor for any hope you have to reach people for Jesus. If you can be a champion for Jewish-Gentile ministry and find other champions in your congregation, it will go a long way to preparing a welcoming place for JGCs to come and work toward spiritual harmony. Any challenges your congregation is willing to face to include people from different cultures will be amply rewarded by the richness of diversity that is part of the beauty of the body of Messiah.

Exercise

1. Are you ready to be a champion for a ministry to JGCs at your church? If so, what action points will you commit to?

2. Do you think your local congregation has what it takes to welcome Jewish-Gentile couples and extend ministry to them?

What are some of the things that your congregation already has that would make it a good place for ministry to JGCs?

What are some of the areas where your church might need help to make JGCs feel at home? What can you do to help address those?

3. Three Scriptures were mentioned as important talking points should you encounter people who doubt whether Jewish people need Jesus to be saved. Would you commit those to memory if you haven't already?

Are there other Scriptures you can think of that would be helpful should the question arise?

Chapter 11
Small Groups for Jewish-Gentile Couple Ministry

What if four to six Jewish-Gentile couples asked you to help them have a safe conversation about spiritual subjects? You would have a readymade small group that could easily become a Havurah!

What's a Havurah?

Havurah (hah-voo-rah) is a Hebrew word that refers to a group of "comrades." Young American Jews who began gathering together took up the term in the 1960s. Dissatisfied with existing Jewish institutions, they were looking to express their Jewish identity in ways that were more open and accepting than the previous European and post-Holocaust experience of their parents. They also wanted to preserve the traditional Jewish idea of community.

Burt Jacobson described the desire of his generation for community beyond the synagogue:

> Many of us are lonely and hunger for meaning beyond our limited selves. We seek genuine fellowship and joy with others, the excitement of encounter with the Transcendent, and the discovery of our roots in the past.[1]

The Havurah developed as an alternate community to function alongside synagogues or Jewish community centers, similar to the "small group" model of many churches. It has become an accepted social structure of American Jewish life. Havurot (plural, rhymes with "Ah you goat") can easily be adapted for groups of Jewish-Gentile couples to explore their cross-cultural challenges, religious beliefs and practical family concerns.

The Havurah is meant to be a shared learning experience where everyone contributes. It's a perfect setting for exploring the struggles that Jewish-Gentile couples face and for sharing the humorous cultural gaffs that all experience.

Most likely you won't have a group of JGCs asking you to help them establish a Havurah, but that doesn't mean that you can't take the initiative to create one. How about offering a Jewish-Gentile couples Havurah as a community service? Ideally you would know at least one Jewish-Gentile couple who would help you contact or seek out others.

The ideas in this chapter are here for you to adapt to your own situation. Tweak my suggestions to fit with your natural gifting or training. Spiritual ministry is a profession, a practice, similar to medicine or law. With time and experience, your wisdom and effectiveness increases. See what you can do to step outside your comfort zone while also being realistic about your abilities.

Discuss the possibilities with others in your ministry situation—perhaps your local congregation, and/or if you are part of an evangelistic organization, talk with your colleagues.

Bringing People Together

Many Jewish-Gentile couples would love to work through their cross-cultural challenges in a friendly, nonjudgmental atmosphere alongside others who know what they're experiencing. There are many ways that you can make it known that you are available to help facilitate that. Post on social media, publish ads in a local newspaper, ask for a few lines in your church's bulletin or a few minutes during the church announcements. If you already know a JGC, ask them to get the word out. And of course, you want to be praying that God will give a little nudge to send people your way.

How about offering a Jewish-Gentile couples Havurah as a community service?

It may seem like nothing is going on. Then it happens. A guy from your fellowship calls to say that he's dating a Jewish girl. A parent contacts you about a daughter who married a wonderful Jewish man, and when you reach out to follow up, she is interested in meeting. You discover neighbors, a Jewish-Gentle couple, who are wondering how to raise their two children. You can tell all these couples that they are the "new normal" in American Jewish life. Or maybe not so new—according to the Jewish intermarriage rate for the past 25 years.

Once you are in conversations with four to six couples like this, invite them to meet others like themselves and to take part in a series of eight meetings as part of a Havurah. Let them know the purpose of the group will be creating understanding between the couples, and to focus on cross-cultural communication so they can better understand one another's identity and spiritual beliefs.

Be sure to let them know at the outset that there is no cost. Present the opportunity with absolutely no pressure or urgency. They get enough of that from one another, parents and in-laws! Suggest that the eight meetings could be held weekly or every other week, to be decided at the first meeting. After eight meetings, the group can decide whether they want to continue to meet.

First Meeting

It is important to set mutually agreed upon expectations during the first meeting. Those expectations should be few and should make everyone comfortable. Is starting and ending the meetings on time an important issue for everyone? How much time would people like to set aside for the group discussion each time, versus hanging out to socialize before or after? A private home is a far better meeting place than an office, but whose home, and by what time should everyone clear out? Do the couples want to take turns bringing snacks or does everyone want to bring a little nosh to share? (Food is essential to any Havurah so you'll want to be sure to put out a nice little spread the first time.)

A ground rule or two for discussion is also important. Each person needs to know they will not be judged for expressing their own views or cultural preferences. The group should agree on best practices for showing respect for one another and be kind and good-natured about holding one another to those.

See what you can do to step outside your comfort zone while also being realistic about your abilities.

In addition to establishing a few ground rules, the first meeting is a good time for people to "air" their own presuppositions/ position. I usually say something brief about my own ethnic background and spiritual conviction.

However, I try to make sure ahead of time that Jewish partners in particular know that I'm a Messianic Jew and that I serve with Jews for Jesus. I don't want anyone to feel ambushed or trapped. I'll reiterate who I am briefly at that first meeting and make sure everyone knows that the group is not intended to be a conversion class. We do, however, aim to create new understanding, which can result in someone having a change of heart. That's up to the individual.

All the couples should introduce themselves, and you might plan a quick "ice breaker" to put people at ease with one another.

Reiterate that the purpose of the group is to create understanding about our cross-cultural differences. Those issues will touch on identity, cross-cultural communication and the couples' differing spiritual beliefs. You will want to announce that at every meeting. Participants need help to stay focused on the purposes of their meetings. Those purposes serve as boundaries for the conversations and build safety into the discussions. Participants will come to own and repeat those purposes to one another.

Setting the Agenda

You'll want to involve all the participants in setting the agenda for discussion.

I asked a group of six Jewish-Gentile couples for ideas on what they would like to discuss in our Havurah. As I listened to their interests, I wrote them down. I tried to organize their ideas into topical groupings. Not everyone had the same level of interest. Gentiles were generally fascinated by everything Jewish, including holidays and religious practices. Jewish partners were not as eager to investigate Christian beliefs. It took some doing to find subjects of interest to all. At the end of this chapter, you'll see the list of nine subject areas that they came up with. Many will be familiar topics that you've just been reading about.

The list isn't meant for you to determine topics for your Havurah; again, the participants need to be able to express their own interests. But it's likely that the list will be similar to the one I've provided. If you ask for suggested topics and a long silence follows because no one wants to be the first to speak up, you can prime the pump with a topic from the list. "What about _____? Would that be of interest?"

You'll want to involve all the participants in setting the agenda for discussion.

You can also ask:

What are some terms that we should define to facilitate our cross-cultural discussions?

Are there any words or concepts that you do not understand when your partner talks about their faith or cultural identity?

Which of his/her cultural or religious practices do you not understand?

What do you wish you could ask about Christian beliefs?

What do you wish you could ask about Jewish beliefs?

Are there any other related concerns or questions that you'd like to see answered during our gatherings?

As you listen to their responses, be sure to take good notes!

Deciding Discussion Topics

Before the next meeting, compile a list of possible discussion topics from the words, concepts, practices, beliefs and related concerns or questions the group came up with. Make a copy for all the participants.

When the group reconvenes, distribute the list and ask each person to check off a certain number of items as their top areas of interest. The top vote-getters will become your subjects for upcoming discussions, with everyone having some ownership of the agenda.

As the group host or facilitator, it's up to you to do your homework ahead of time. Get familiar with the topics and terms. Everyone should have a turn at saying what, if anything, the words mean to them, but as translator, you'll need to use your turn to give a very clear and simple explanation or definition for each of the topics. You'll find many of them in this book, but not all. You might need to look for some terms in a dictionary or an online website and the Bible. It is important to identify your sources, and don't presume that everyone is going to see them all as equally credible.

Your Role

Remember that your role is the facilitator or host. You are responsible for encouraging and guiding discussions while building trust within the group by keeping the conversations open and nonjudgmental. You are not there to provide all the answers.

As you encourage each participant to share their point of view and to listen to those of others, you will be modeling how a good listener interacts. Others will see that they can explain themselves and their differences with grace, mutual respect and hopefully some humor.

In other words, you want to create an environment where all of the partners feel that their cultural perspectives are heard and respected. Hearing one another doesn't mean that they have to agree on all the issues.

While a Havurah is a good tool for creating a safe community for exploring difficult or new spiritual subjects, the aim is actually pre-evangelistic for the most part. You have offered to help couples create understanding through effective cross-cultural communication—and you don't want to employ a "bait and switch" tactic.

Pre-evangelistic doesn't mean it excludes any evangelistic conversation. Of course you can introduce elements of gospel truth when someone asks a question that makes it appropriate to do so. I find that it builds trust with the group if I request their permission to answer such questions. You want to be careful that one of the Christians doesn't toss you a "softball." I've had partners ask me a question they know the answer to because they want someone else to make a gospel statement to their spouse. Guard against pushing your or someone else's evangelistic agenda by sticking to the agreed-upon aim of the group.

You want to create an environment where all of the partners feel that their cultural perspectives are heard and respected.

Pre-evangelistic efforts can lead to opportunities to present spiritual truth. And that is an incredible privilege of Jewish-Gentile couple ministry. The Havurah is one appropriate structure for creating clarity and understanding that can lead someone into knowing God.

If you are hearing or sensing spiritual openness from someone who doesn't yet know Jesus, offer to meet with him or her separately to discuss the gospel. I have found that visits with individual Jewish people (or along with their Gentile partners) tend to be the most fruitful for their spiritual discovery.

What to Expect

No two groups are the same, frankly because people are so different. That's the adventure of this sort of ministry. Still, some things are pretty much bound to happen in ministry to Jewish-Gentile couples.

You can expect that some people will unintentionally make statements that others find offensive or culturally ignorant. Make sure to warn people early on that understanding our cultural differences can be an uncomfortable experience. A little discomfort is a small price to pay for a place where people can grow in their appreciation for other cultures and ideas. The Havurah is a shared opportunity for learning by a small community of couples with a unique experience. It requires a degree of patience and acceptance.

And then there are people who will intentionally ask provocative questions. For them, the experience can be more like a game. There is the person who asks, "So, you think I'm going to hell if I don't believe in Jesus?" Whatever you do, don't respond with "yes" or "no" for the answer! That isn't dealing with the real question—or in some cases, the statement behind the question.

Probe a little by asking a clarifying question in response. Like, "Do you really believe in a concept or a place called 'hell'?" In almost every instance, the questioner will honestly admit that they don't believe in hell, particularly if they are Jewish. I usually respond, "Then, I guess the question is really irrelevant, isn't it? Let's talk about something else that does matter." It isn't said as a judgment or an accusation.

And then there are people who will intentionally ask provocative questions.

Some people ask off-putting questions to avoid dealing with subjects that make them feel uncomfortable. They might be amused by causing others discomfort or they might be trying to justify their perception that another person's view is intolerant. You don't need to address any of those subtexts, just understand that they might exist beneath such a question.

Creating a safe environment for conversation can be like turning a light on so others can see what's happening in the conversation.

Again, sometimes, in order to get at underlying truth, we need to defer a discussion to a more personal conversation outside of the group. Don't hesitate to ask someone who is becoming spiritually vulnerable to hold on to their really good question or thought for a private time after the meeting. The host or facilitator is responsible to be aware of the boundaries so as to preserve discretion and safety for the participants.

How Do You Facilitate a Havurah Discussion?

Okay, you've gathered a Havurah or small group. The group has chosen their topics and you're ready to begin.

Much of what you'll do employs practices you learned at the beginning of this book—asking the various participants what certain words or phrases mean to them, asking clarifying questions, making sure everyone is heard, offering an "outside" objective definition that might help to reconcile some of those differences of understanding. (That's where you'll come in having looked up these words and ideas as mentioned earlier.)

Some people ask off-putting questions to avoid dealing with subjects that make them feel uncomfortable.

Your role as the group's cross-cultural interpreter will also help people to express their questions or ideas in culturally relevant ways. For example if someone asks, "What is worship like in a Jewish church?" You (the interpreter) respond: "Jewish church? Maybe you mean to say a synagogue or temple?" and/or "Can you describe what you have in mind when you say 'worship'?" Show the others how to ask clarifying questions respectfully. Help people to not fear being probed for the sake of creating understanding.

Aim to keep definitions simple but clear. Sometimes people define a word with a similar undefined term or phrase. For example, someone might say, "Christianity is what I believe about Christ." We don't know what the person believes about Christ, so we still don't know what Christianity means to them. Just be careful that you don't let the discussion get "too far off in the weeds."

Make a distinction between traditional views and objective presentation. Protect people who may end up feeling foolish as a result of their lack of exposure to different perspectives. For example, Christians wonder why Jewish people can't see that Isaiah 53 speaks clearly about the Messiah Jesus. However, rabbis teach with much academic creativity that the passage is about the people of Israel and not Jesus. That's a traditional view that is called into question when a Jewish person reads the passage in context.

As you encourage and guide conversations, keep reminding everyone that it is a learning opportunity to be shared in a small community. Keep the atmosphere safe and nonjudgmental. If you can do that, you'll know you're succeeding as participants are free to express what they think and confess what they don't understand. When you start hearing expressions of appreciation for new discoveries, you'll know that you are all engaged in a successful experience together. That builds community and feeds the atmosphere of freedom for discussion and mutual respect.

How Do You Wrap Up a Havurah?

During the last agreed upon meeting, take time to review what people have learned. Invite them to share, "What are your new cross-cultural understandings? What has become clear to you? What do you understand better about the beliefs/identity of your partner?"

You might want to ask if they would like to continue meeting, and for how many more discussions. You can also offer to schedule follow-up conversations with any individuals or couples, based on their interest in finding spiritual harmony.

Spiritual awakening is often a messy and unpredictable process. We can't control it, but God can, and He does! His Spirit is wiser and far more creative than we are. So you can trust Him to lead for the next steps.

***

List of topics:

1. Identity issues

a. *Jewish*, *Israel* and *Chosen People*: What's the difference between those terms?

b. Gentile

c. Christian

d. What is the identity of a child from a Jewish-Gentile couple?

2. Christian distinctions—what are:

a. Fundamentalists

b. Evangelicals

c. Denominations

d. Catholics

e. "Christian" offshoot groups like Mormons and Jehovah Witnesses

f. Jewish views of Christians

g. A Jewish view of Christian history

h. Implications of the phrase "Christians and Jews" [Hint: it communicates mutual exclusion and a false dichotomy by contrasting a religious category with an ethnic one.]

3. Jesus (aka "the 'J' word")

a. Traditional Jewish views and sensibilities about Jesus

b. Christian understanding of Jesus

c. Biblical material related to Jesus

4. Salvation

a. Christian understanding of terms like *sin*, *repentance* and *conversion*

b. Jewish perspectives of terms like *sin*, *repentance* and *t'shuvah*

5. Problem of evil in a world that a good God created

a. What's the point of believing anything?

b. Different views on dealing with suffering

6. Intermarriage

a. Jewish community issues – outreach, spousal conversion, marginalization

b. Christian community issues – being unequally yoked

c. Your experience of guilt, fear and shame

7. Views of heaven and hell

a. Jewish perspectives on the grave and beyond

b. Christian beliefs and what matters

8. Sovereignty of God and free will of humanity

9. Finding spiritual harmony

Conclusion

If you are still reading this chapter, there's a good chance you are interested in facilitating a Jewish-Gentile couples Havurah. Mazel tov! I know from experience that it can be a rewarding experience and lead to some great ministry opportunities. If you are thinking you are not suited for this particular opportunity, skip to the next chapter. Otherwise, complete the exercise below.

Exercise

Begin praying now for those God will bring to the JGC couples Havurah you are hoping to host. In the next few days, share your vision with others you can enlist to pray for you.

List six things you can do to get out the word that you are looking to start a Havurah for Jewish-Gentile couples. Give yourself a timeline to do each of them . . . and continue to pray!

1. ____________________

2. ____________________

3. ____________________

4. ____________________

5. ____________________

6. ____________________

1. Richard Siegel, Michael Strassfeld and Sharon Strassfeld, eds. *The Jewish Catalog: But Do It Yourself Kit* (Philadelphia: Jewish Publication Society of America, 1973), 280–281.

Chapter 12
Connecting through Social and Cultural Events

Jewish events and occasions can be meaningful relationship-building times for JGCs, and can also lead to conversations about spiritual truth. The following pages suggest practical ideas for several of these occasions. If you're part of a Messianic congregation or Jewish ministry, you are already familiar with these events and opportunities. You might want to skim the chapter for any nuances that might add to what you are already doing.

Remember that social events are opportunities to build relationships and trust. Take time to get to know and get comfortable with people without the pressure to bring up spiritual truths. Keep in mind that when people from different backgrounds experience cultural events together, someone is going to have moments and experiences that are unfamiliar and potentially confusing or uncomfortable. Try to leave time and opportunity to discuss those during or after the event.

Shabbat Dinners

A Friday night Shabbat (Sabbath) gathering is a wonderful social setting for relational ministry and spiritual discussions. It is traditionally a family time, and a time to welcome friends as well. It can also be a good time for a Havurah.

Typically people gather just before sundown, though some might come earlier in the day to help with dinner preparations; it depends if the hosting family is providing the dinner or if it's a larger group with others sharing the cooking responsibility. Part of the joy is involving as many people as possible. Some might prepare food or help set the room and table. Others might drop by a store for last-minute needs or take time to choose a psalm to read at table. All of that "pre-activity" helps to create a family-like atmosphere.

The evening doesn't need a heavy structure or a lot of religious ritual. Shabbat is the time to slow down from the ordinary activity of the week to rest in the goodness of the Lord and take time to appreciate Him. If you are hosting, do what you can to quiet yourself and the home so the evening is easy and simple.

A nice way to begin is for someone to say the traditional blessing over two Shabbat candles with everyone gathered around as they are lit at sundown. According to the Jewish calendar, the day ends as the sun goes down and the new day begins after it has set. Having everyone gather to observe that transition symbolizes the group is entering into the Shabbat rest.

Once the candles are lit, you might also have someone say the traditional blessings over a cup of wine and challah (Sabbath bread). Usually after the blessing for the bread, part of the loaf is passed among the guests to tear off and enjoy a piece. You might also recite a prayer that gives thanks to God for Sabbath rest. A good resource to learn the melodies as well as the words to these prayers is: http://www.sidduraudio.com/.

A Shabbat dinner is a perfect opportunity to build community—it's a family event around home and food and fellowship. The spiritual theme of Sabbath is rest, and naturally lends to a casual and relaxed time together. Many secular Jews enjoy this time for its cultural and social aspects, while recognizing and respecting the fact that others will connect to it on a spiritual level as well. So now it's time to eat. A Christian or Messianic Jew might ordinarily say a table grace at the beginning of the meal. Jewish custom is to offer a liturgical prayer at the end. Many secular Jews and Gentiles don't pray at all. So as people take their seats around the dinner table, can you pray before eating when some of guests will not be accustomed to that? Sure, so long as you take a moment to ensure it doesn't make anyone uncomfortable.

The spiritual theme of Sabbath is rest, and naturally lends to a casual and relaxed time together.

As mentioned in chapter 8, I always let dinner guests know that I'm about to take a moment to thank God for His blessings before we eat. I tell them, "This is something we usually do as a family, but we don't want you to feel imposed upon. We are glad you are with us, but if you want to go to your own happy place while we pray that's fine too. We just want you to be comfortable. Let's pray."

What are the origins of celebrating the Sabbath? The Lord wanted His Israelite people to remember that He rested from His creation effort in the very beginning. How did God rest? He wasn't dirty, sweaty or tired from His labor. And He didn't run into creator's block, suddenly unable to think of anything else to create. The Hebrew text said God rested because everything that He'd made was exactly as He wanted it. In fact, He called it "very good." God rested in His own sufficiency, and He asks us to do the same thing, that is, to rest in His sufficiency (and not our own).

It is refreshing to remember that we live by faith, trusting daily in God's love for us. We can rest from trying to please God or earn His favor. I find it so refreshing to rest in the knowledge that God loves me deeply enough to have sent His Son the Messiah to do for us what we could not do for ourselves.

So, the aim of the evening is spiritual refreshment. An elaborate meal isn't necessary.

The evening naturally lends itself to a brief reading from a Thanksgiving psalm at the table. After the meal, in keeping with the spiritual theme, it would be appropriate to read a Bible passage and then discuss it together.

When inviting guests, let them know the social and spiritual purpose of the evening. Encourage your Jewish guests to share some of their own Shabbat memories around the table. And as they leave, be sure to wish everyone "Shabbat Shalom," Sabbath peace.

Holiday Celebrations

Passover

Passover is the first of the annual feasts that God commanded the children of Israel to celebrate. It goes to the very heart of who God is: our powerful and gracious Redeemer who sets us free so that we can be in relationship with Him. Like Shabbat, Passover is celebrated by religious and secular Jews alike and is a joyous affirmation of Jewish identity.

Seder (say-der) is the Hebrew term for the Passover meal and all the traditional liturgy that comes with it. Many families abbreviate the liturgy and focus on the meal. If you plan a Passover seder in your home, you can go easy on the liturgy if you want, but you'll want to be sure to mention that this is a time to recall how God delivered the Israelites from slavery in Egypt. There are traditional food items on the table that help tell the story of Passover, and the family and guests normally partake of them together with a long or short explanation of their meaning. Likewise, each person drinks four times from their own cup of wine (or grape juice if substitution is needed).

This remembrance continues with His followers today as we celebrate communion.

Matzah or unleavened bread is also a key element of the celebration, and you'll want to be sure that all the food you serve for Passover is free of any leaven (baking soda, baking powder or yeast of any kind).

This festival of redemption also has special meaning for Christians as Jesus celebrated it with His disciples just before He sacrificed His life for us. While the themes of redemption and the Passover lamb speak to us of physical redemption from slavery and freedom from the tyranny of foreign rulers, we also see a clear foreshadowing of spiritual redemption, and freedom from sin and self-serving habits. Jesus' atoning sacrifice set us free to know and love God as we were meant to. In fact, when Jesus celebrated Passover as His "last supper" He indicated that the ceremonial bread and wine pointed to His body and blood, and that His followers should remember Him each time they partook of them. This remembrance continues with His followers today as we celebrate communion.

If you live near a Jews for Jesus branch or local Messianic congregation, you and any Jewish-Gentile couples you know would be most welcome to celebrate with us. If you live far from any branch or congregation and would like to put together a holiday celebration of your own, we can help provide liturgy and recipes. Our website, www.jewsforjesus.org, has a wealth of information about this and other Jewish holidays, including traditional Jewish understandings as well as Messianic interpretations that show meaningful connections to Christian beliefs. You can also contact our headquarters.

The High Holidays

The Jewish High Holy Days, or fall festivals, are also terrific occasions for providing spiritual ministry to Jewish-Gentile couples and their families. Our Jews for Jesus branch in Los Angeles partners with local Messianic congregations and churches to create welcoming services during the High Holy Days. Whereas synagogues traditionally charge a price for tickets to attend High Holy Day services, we are able to provide meaningful ministry free of charge. Messianic Jews as well as Jewish seekers and their families attend these services.

The two main festivals of the season are Rosh Hashanah, which the Bible calls the Day for Blowing Trumpets and Yom Kippur, the Day of Atonement. They fall on the first and the tenth day of the Hebrew month of Tishrai, the seventh month in the Jewish calendar year. Some years the holidays fall in September, others, October. If you don't have your own Jewish calendar, it's very easy to look up the dates on the Internet.

Have a few mature Jewish believers present who can help welcome the Jewish partners to the service.

A JGC's attendance at our services might indicate the Jewish partner's openness to finding spiritual harmony with their Gentile partner, though the only way to know is to have a conversation with him or her. If you don't live near a Jews for Jesus branch or Messianic congregation, again, you might consider putting together your own event if you have enough people who are interested to help. You might see about using your church's facilities.

Some have questioned whether holding a High Holiday service in a church would present cultural barriers to Jewish partners (think of the 12 Cultural Signal Systems, and cultural symbols like a cross or a stained-glass window). In my opinion, Jewish people who, through intermarriage, have already disaffiliated from a very traditional form of Judaism shouldn't have a problem with a Messianic service. It would be no surprise that Jesus is going to be included.

Adequate advertising and personally inviting Jewish-Gentile couples you know are both key to the success of the High Holy Day events. You'll also want to have a few mature Jewish believers present who can help welcome the Jewish partners to the service. Jews tend to feel more comfortable if we see other Jews visibly involved in the service. It's like finding a good Chinese restaurant. When you look in the window, if you see mostly Asian faces enjoying the food you know that it's probably going to be a pretty good place.

At Rosh Hashanah, be sure to have someone who can blow the shofar (ram's horn/trumpet). A traditional Scripture reading for this holiday is referred to as the *Akeda* (ah-kay-duh), which means "the binding." The story of Abraham's faith as demonstrated in Genesis 22:1–19 is powerful. For believers in Jesus it represents a foreshadowing of God sending His own Son as a substitute, just as He provided the ram in the thicket as a substitute for Abraham's son.

In Jewish culture, Rosh Hashanah is considered the Jewish New Year. A Rosh Hashanah event should have a substantial table prepared for nosh (snacks) and fellowship afterwards. Traditional holiday fare includes honey cakes, slices of apple and bowls of honey for dipping and a variety of sweets to help usher in a sweet new year.

Yom Kippur, the Day of Atonement, is all about God's forgiveness of sin. It is a perfect opportunity to explain the gospel of salvation in Messiah Jesus. Since Yom Kippur is a day of fasting, a service would not normally be followed by refreshments.

Books like *Walk with Yeshua Through the Jewish Year* (a children's book by Janie-sue Wertheim and Kathy Shapiro), as well as Barney Kasden's *God's Appointed Times* and Martha Zimmerman's *Celebrating Biblical Feasts: In Your Home or Church*, all provide ideas for appropriate cultural and spiritual celebrations.

Jewish greeting cards can also be a very good bridge for Gentile partners to reach out to Jewish in-laws.

Holiday Cards

Jewish holiday cards are appreciated as a kind and appropriate social gesture for connecting with people throughout the seasons. Passover, Rosh Hashanah and Hanukkah are especially good occasions to send greeting cards. Take the opportunity to build relationships and express cross-cultural appreciation to the Jewish-Gentile couples you know. Jewish greeting cards can also be a very good bridge for Gentile partners to reach out to Jewish in-laws. The Jewish partner may or may not think to send a card, but if the Gentile partner says, "Look, I picked up this Happy Passover card for your mom and dad, want to sign it with me?" it can go a long way.

You can purchase appropriate seasonal cards from card shops or wherever you usually find them.[1] I begin planning to send cards a month before the holiday. I prefer the cards to arrive during the week preceding the actual holiday. It is completely appropriate to send greeting cards to unbelievers and to include a word of "blessing."

Holiday themes lend themselves to express spiritual thoughts. Passover celebrates God's grace as a powerful Redeemer. An appropriate phrase is, "Give thanks to the Lord for he is good; and his loving-kindness endures forever." That appears throughout the Psalms and especially in the six praise psalms read at Passover.

Rosh Hashanah cards traditionally focus on wishing others a sweet New Year. However, it is good to include a simple word of blessing or shalom. The card can convey cross-cultural sensitivity and thoughtfulness.

Hanukkah is an interesting holiday, as the only biblical mention of it is found in the New Testament; see John 10:22ff. The Feast of Dedication is a celebration of national survival and victory over enemies of the Jews who imposed religious oppression. Traditional Hanukkah cards mention the themes of light, joy and sweetness. You can include your own Bible references in the card, especially if they mention light. Some examples:

> The LORD is my light and my salvation;
> Whom shall I fear?
> The LORD is the strength of my life;
> Of whom shall I be afraid. (Psalm 27:1)
>
> For with You is the fountain of life;
> In Your light we see light." (Psalm 36:9)

If appropriate—that is, if the Jewish partner has shown that she or he does not object to hearing quotes from the New Testament—you could also inscribe words from a verse like John 8:12:

> I am the light of the world. He who follows Me shall not walk in darkness, but have the light of life. (John 8:12)

Since we are talking about Jewish-Gentile couple ministry, you can certainly include holiday cards for the season of the Resurrection (Easter) and the Messiah's birth (Advent or Christmas). I suggest religious cards that include a Bible verse or write in one of your own choosing for expressing a spiritual testimony.

It is completely appropriate to send greeting cards to unbelievers and to include a word of "blessing."

Interfaith Bar/Bat Mitzvah Preparation and Celebration

These life-cycle events provide opportunities for JGCs to appreciate one another's identities and can also be a time for you to express friendship and affirmation of both cultures.

Some Messianic congregations provide bar (for boys) and bat (for girls) mitzvah training and also conduct services as a rite of passage for children and a testimony to families. I encourage Jewish missionary staff members who are comfortable chanting traditional synagogue prayers to prepare children of Jewish-Gentile couples for bar and bat mitzvah services. If that's you, in the course of training you will have opportunities to discuss spiritual, religious and especially identity matters with the children. Remember that you need both parents to agree to any spiritual training you provide their children.

These celebrations can be excellent testimonies to relatives and friends of the Jewish-Gentile couple. Bar/bat mitzvah ceremonies also validate the children as remaining part of the Jewish people. A child can be proficient in the traditional prayers and liturgy without denying faith in Messiah Jesus.

Also, since the bar or bat mitzvah child reads a portion of the Scriptures for the celebration, you have an opportunity to disciple that child as you study the Scriptures together. Lessons can also include the parents if they want to learn traditional Jewish practices with their child. They, too, can join the conversation about the Bible.

Children and Bible Study

Bible clubs are a wonderful way to help introduce children to the Scriptures and enculturate them in Jewish biblical heritage. Many Jewish-Gentile couple parents welcome an after school Bible club for their children. They appreciate the spiritual partnership, especially when the teacher is someone skilled in communicating biblical truth to children.

Many Jewish-Gentile couple parents welcome an after school Bible club for their children.

Messianic congregations and missions, including our branch in Israel, offer Bible clubs for grammar school-aged children with great success. Along with skilled teachers, it is important to have excellent curricula. Contact the Jews for Jesus Children's and Youth Ministry (CYM) for help in offering good curricula. It is important to ask both parents to give their signed permission indicating informed consent for us to provide spiritual training to their children.

Bible Reading with and to Children

One of the most effective ways to introduce children to spiritual truth is by reading the Bible to them and with them. I encourage parents to take on this ministry, especially if they are not familiar with the Bible. One or both parents can do this, but be sure that they are able to collaborate. If children sense that there is tension associated with the Bible, they could take a negative impression of it. You wouldn't them to feel that the Bible somehow made Mommy and Daddy angry with each other.

Some of my warmest parenting memories with our own children are of times spent reading the Bible to them at bedtime. Whenever we finished a story, I would close the Bible and pray for them. That investment in their spiritual growth has returned dividends beyond measure.

Children's Camps

Numerous Messianic congregations and Jewish ministries have provided quality camp ministries for children. These camps deliver Jewish enculturation and a Jesus-centered spiritual discipleship.

I'm most familiar with Jews for Jesus Camp Gilgal program, which my own kids attended as campers and later as camp counselors, because they'd loved it so much and wanted to "give back." The sense of community these camps foster is amazing, as is the spiritual care and attention campers receive there. Some of the campers are from Messianic homes; others are from homes where only one parent is a believer, including a number of Jewish-Gentile families. With full permission from the parents, an untold number of children who've attended have come to faith in the Messiah Jesus over the years.

Information about those camps is available from the Jews for Jesus website at www.jewsforjesus.org/join/gilgal.

For further examples and information concerning Jewish life-cycle events and social occasions, see appendix 7.

Resources for Learning Jewish Culture

I've been describing social and cultural structures or events that lend themselves to engaging Jewish-Gentile couples in spiritual ministry. I also want to suggest social and cultural events and resources where you can learn more about Jewish culture. The more you experience and know about Jewish life, the better prepared you'll be for cross-cultural conversations. Some of the following will also be appropriate venues to promote your Jewish-Gentile couples' ministry, or meet JGCs who will be interested in what you have to offer.

Fairs and Cultural Events

Attending Jewish community fairs and Israeli and Jewish cultural events is a fun way to learn about contemporary Jewish life. They can be rich experiences for Jewish-Gentile couples who want to participate in the culture of the broader Jewish community and/or pass on Jewish identity to children.

The Getty Center Museum in Westwood, near UCLA, hosted an exhibition titled, "Too Jewish? Varieties of Jewish Expression in America." A group of us from the Jews for Jesus staff in Los Angeles attended, and some of our children came with us. A few of the adults actually wore clothing that identified us as Jews for Jesus. I think we actually became part of the exhibit that evening! We had some interesting conversations with other attendees.

Depending on your city, local Jewish communities offer celebrations like Jerusalem Day, A Jewish Book Festival and Israel Independence Day. These fairs often feature booths, music and dance, public speakers and sometimes a parade. Watch also for various Jewish community cultural-awareness events. They often take place around a holiday or a political issue that touches on current Jewish or Israeli interests.

You might even be able to pay for and set up a booth for outreach to Jewish-Gentile couples. This should be presented as a service where resources are offered to the Jewish public and in particular as a welcome to Jewish-Gentile couples, their families and children. Jewish event sponsors / community leaders might object, but you never know. It is worth asking. If you can get a space, it's a great pre-evangelistic initiative. It gives you a chance to meet JGCs you probably wouldn't otherwise connect with.

Print Resources

In many countries, and certainly in the United States, Jewish newspapers are published, often weekly, in many cities with large Jewish populations. You could find the *Jewish Journal* of Southern California, *The Jewish Times* or *Jewish Week* of New York, the Washington *Jewish Week* and the Philadelphia *Jewish Exponent* to name a few. If you don't live in any of those cities, or if you just prefer to avoid the newsprint, you can also find online versions. In addition, there are international newspapers from Israel like *The Jerusalem Post*.

Jewish interest magazines are also great resources to have your finger on the pulse of American Jewish culture. The are usually available online, and include *MOMENT* or *COMMENTARY*, *Hadassah Women's Zionist Organization of America*, *Heeb*, *Jewish World Review*, *Reform Judaism*, *Tablet* and *Tikkun*. Each one presents a different slice of the American Jewish perspective. You might see advertisements for Christian tour groups in these periodicals. Advertisers are aware that Christians are interested in Jewish culture and read the magazines to catch up on current events. If you are interested in reaching out to Jewish people, what they think about and care about will be of interest to you.

If you aren't aware of the published resources in your area, check out a website for a synagogue or synagogues near you. Very often they promote articles from a local Jewish paper, a favorite website or magazine.

Online Resources
The Jerusalem Post publishes articles online at www.jpost.com.

Another Israeli source, *Ynet,* can be found at www.ynetnews.com.

Arutz Sheva (Channel 7) is an online Israeli news service at www.israelnationalnews.com. It's also available on a smart phone app.

J-street, found at www.jstreet.org, is a popular online resource.

Jewish Telegraphic Agency is the primary resource for Jewish news. You can find it at www.jta.org.

Popular webzines which provide contemporary information include the *Tablet* which is found at www.tabletmag.com and *Heeb* magazine which can be found at www.heebmagazine.com. These offer alternative, often edgy, views about contemporary Jewish life in America and Israel.

The Messianic Times provides information about the Messianic community and news from Israel. It can be found at www.messianictimes.com.

Almost all of the American Jewish mission agencies, including Jews for Jesus, provide outreach and update information through their own websites.

Christian Newspapers
Some cities have local Christian newspapers, which can be wonderful vehicles for offering services to Jewish-Gentile couples and their children. (As can the religious pages of secular newspapers.) If you have small groups, holiday services or other resources that are specifically geared to welcome Jewish people, consider advertising in a local newspaper, be it secular or Christian.

You might try offering a resource with an ad that says, "Jewish-Gentile couples welcome: Discover an alternative to conversion classes and find a place where you can discover God without losing your Jewish identity or your love for Jesus."

Social Media

Jews for Jesus hosts a website at www.jewishgentilecouples.com as well as a Facebook fan page also called "Jewish-Gentile Couples." It is very easy to advertise on Facebook with a small budget, and you can set up your own regional fan page to reach JGCs. Facebook has filters that reach specific age groups and geographic areas. Using appropriate meta tags, it is possible to connect with a specific audience. Try #Jewish, #intermarried, #jewsandgentilesmarried, and add another that includes your city or town along with one of the above examples.

Those are just a few ideas for learning more about Jewish culture and contemporary issues. I'd love to hear from you if you have ideas or experiences that have been a help to you. I'm also interested in what you might discover about other outreach sources where you have made Jewish-Gentile couple or intermarriage ministry available in your community.

Conclusion

Cultural and life-cycle events are important experiences for JGCs to share. Discussing them can become part of the process of creating understanding and appreciation for the differences between their cultures.

If you want to reach out to Jewish-Gentile couples, it's a good idea for you to take opportunities to experience and appreciate Jewish culture as well. These experiences will not only help you understand Jewish people, they will help you meet Jewish people.

Exercise

Take time to find out this year's dates for Passover, Rosh Hashanah, and Hanukkah and mark them on your calendar. Make a list of people you'd like to send greeting cards to, and give yourself a two-week reminder before each holiday so you'll have plenty of time to shop for and send your cards.

Consider printing a small number of cards that offer your services as someone who is available to promote cross-cultural understanding between Jewish-Gentile couples. You never know when you might meet someone in passing who will be interested, or how much time you'll have to exchange information.

A Word of Encouragement

These twelve chapters are just the beginning! As you prayerfully connect with Jewish-Gentile couples, you are sure to continue learning and discovering ways to build understanding. God bless you as you step out in faith, and may you have the joy of seeing the couples you care for find spiritual harmony through the Messiah Jesus.

1. If you normally send e-cards for the holidays, Jews for Jesus provides a selection of those for free, along with articles and various resources concerning these special days: http://jewsforjesus.org/judaica.

Appendices

Appendix 1: Words Related to Jewish Identity

The "basic vocabulary" in chapter 2 includes words to help you understand issues of Jewish identity. Following are some nuances to help you further understand those issues, both historically, and as they relate to contemporary Jewish identity.

Jewish Ethnicity

Biblical view

In the Bible, Jewish ethnicity is most often identified through the father. Genealogical lists provide the names of male ancestors for a tribe, clan or family. So, Abraham is identified as the father of Isaac who was the father of Jacob (Israel).

The New Testament pattern follows Jewish practice continuing the same line of patrilineal descent. In the Gospel of Matthew (Matthew 1:1–17) the genealogical descent for Messiah Jesus is introduced as "the genealogy of Jesus Christ [the Messiah], the Son of David, the Son of Abraham."

And yet, women are occasionally mentioned as key figures in ethnic lineage. Four women are mentioned in Matthew's ancestry of Jesus. One of the women was Ruth the Moabite wife of Boaz. Their son, Obed, was the father of Jesse, who was the father of King David in the line of the Messiah Jesus. So Gentiles, like Ruth the Moabite and Uriah the Hittite, did not negate the ethnicity of a Jewish king. Neither did it invalidate the Jewishness of Jesus the Messiah, a descendent of King David.

Rabbinic view

Rabbis' opinions about who is a Jew have accumulated and changed over two thousand years, and reflect culture and customs. Many take the position that Jewishness is transmitted through the mother (matrilineal descent) as opposed to the traditional patrilineal descent that is normative in the Bible.

The State of Israel's view

Today, any Jewish person arriving in the State of Israel may request, and be granted, Israeli citizenship under the Law of Return. People merely have to prove that they are Jewish by virtue of having had at least one Jewish grandparent. Genealogy, not adherence to the religion of Judaism, is required.

However, under current Israeli law, exclusion from citizenship status has been made possible based on a Jewish person having "converted to another religion." That exclusion is defined by two amendments to the Law of Return as applying specifically to a Jewish immigrant who previously became a follower of Messiah Jesus. In that unique case, Jewish ethnicity is regarded as voided for the purpose of considering Israeli citizenship.

Jew

Technically, and for the purposes of this workbook, *Jew* is an ethnic term; yet people use the word to mean many different things.

In 2001 the National Jewish Population Survey (NJPS) took a religious definition for who is a Jew. To be included in that study, a person had to hold Judaism as their exclusive religious faith. Ethnicity didn't matter. In contrast to that, the 2001 American Jewish Identity Survey (AJIS) included ethnic Jews who reported "no religion" or a secular outlook. That (AJIS) study came out with a higher figure of Jewish population for the same period than the NJPS—by about 300,000 people.

In 2002, the San Francisco Institute for Jewish and Community Research (IJCR) survey took a sociological approach. It asked about "Jewish connections" rather than religious orientation. It reported an even greater number of American Jewish people, nearly 6.7 million, compared to at least a million fewer in the other surveys during the same time period.

Contemporary studies show that the majority of American Jews do not define themselves by religious attachment to Judaism. More than 63 percent of American Jews are not affiliated with any synagogue or Jewish social institution. Demographer of American Jewry, Gary Tobin, observed, "Jews are not disappearing, they are transforming."

Note: Only the State of Israel has a "legal definition" for Jewish people, and that is due to the rights of citizenship and economic incentives for new Jewish immigrants under the 1950 Law of Return.

Jewish

Jewish culture is as diverse as the many parts of the world where we've been scattered. At least four different words are commonly used to describe Jewish people according to their geographic distinction: *Ashkenazi*, *Sephardi*, *Mizrahi* (also transliterated *Mizrachi*) and *Diaspora*.

Diaspora Jews refers to all Jews who live outside of the State of Israel. *Diaspora* is the Greek word for "scatter" or "disperse." Since the modern establishment of the Jewish homeland, Israeli Jews have spoken of the community remaining in Diaspora as living in the *galut*, Hebrew for "exile," since they choose to remain outside of the now-existing homeland.

Ashkenazi Jewish people were settled in Eastern European countries, like Russia, Poland, Lithuania, Latvia, Belarus, Austria, Hungary, Germany and other parts of Europe. (And don't be surprised to find that there are subgroups even among Ashkenazi Jews!)

Sephardi Jews see their historic origin from a period of Jewish migration to Spain, primarily after the Crusades and up until the fifteenth century. Jews lived in North Africa and on the Iberian Peninsula under Muslim rulers and Catholic kings. They eventually migrated back into North Africa and into the Middle East.

Mizrachi Jews refers to those from the *Mizrach* or "East" in Hebrew. Sometimes they are identified in this way in Israel, as having come from Muslim countries such as Lebanon, Iraq, Yemen, Syria, Iran, and the former Russian Republic in Asia, Afghanistan, Pakistan and India. Note: those same groups sometimes also refer to themselves as *Sephardi*. *Mizrahi* became a more common self-identification with the establishment of the State of Israel, since Israeli Jews are also people of the Middle East.

Jewry

Jewry is a collective term for Jewish people. We speak of "American Jewry," "Russian-speaking Jewry" or "Israeli Jewry." The wider designation is known as "World Jewry."

Judaism

Judaism is considered the traditional monotheistic religion of the Jewish people (as opposed to ethnicity). The religion was derived from rabbinic law that was codified roughly 200–400 years after Jesus, but it has changed a great deal over time and is practiced in diverse ways.

Jewish people use the term broadly, and not always in a religious sense. *Judaism* is sometimes used to describe Jewish civilization and even culture.

Milton Steinberg, in his book *Basic Judaism*, described Judaism as "the total actualities, past and present, of the . . . Jewish people . . . (embracing) secular as well as sacred elements." In that sense, Judaism is like a large pot into which many elements of Jewish life are thrown, like a complex stew of diverse ingredients. That would include religious as well as nonreligious "ingredients."[1]

Rabbi Stephen Wylen, in his introduction to Judaism, defines Judaism as "the way of life of the Jewish people. Culture, customs, ethics, sense of self . . . are part of Judaism as much as the faith and rituals of the Jewish religion."[2] In her personal search for Jewish identity, contemporary writer Lisa Schiffman spoke of her quest as an effort of "working on her Judaism."[3] In a traditional sense, Jewish people use the term *Judaism* very broadly.

The concept of Judaism means so many different things depending on who uses the term that it's no wonder the term can be confusing for a cultural outsider. In fact, the word can sometimes confuse rather than create understanding when trying to communicate about one's Jewish identity.

---

1. Milton Steinberg, *Basic Judaism* (New York: Harcourt, Brace & World, Inc., 1947), 3.
2. Stephen Wylen, *Settings of Silver: An Introduction to Judaism* (Mahwah, NJ: Paulest Press, 1989), 3.
3. Lisa Schiffman, *Generation J* (San Francisco: Harper Collins, 2000), 156–7.

Appendix 2: The Purpose and Promise of Jewish Survival

This appendix speaks to the biblical perspective of something that is central to Jewish identity: the deep concern for Jewish people to survive.

The Jewish survival instinct is powerful and at times mysterious, given the reality that among Jewish people there is no one agreed upon idea of exactly what it means for us to survive as a people. Neither is there agreement on how or why we have survived thus far against all odds, or whether there is some "bigger purpose" for our future as a people.

Perhaps the one thing that Jewish people can agree on when it comes to survival is our response to anything that is viewed as a threat to the existence of our people.

In the past, North American Jewish leaders spoke out against Jewish intermarriage because it was almost always seen as a direct threat to Jewish survival. Since the sociological shift in the 1990s, the Jewish community has debated whether intermarriage is good for the Jews or bad for the Jews. At first the general sentiment remained consistent with the past perception, that intermarriage is very bad for the Jews because it poses a threat to our survival.

However, over the past 25 years, efforts to attract disaffiliated Jewish people back to traditional Judaism have mostly failed, including those who have intermarried. So efforts are made to bring Gentile partners into big tent Judaism. That opens up the issue of whether Gentiles need to convert to Judaism or whether they can be part of a religiously Jewish community without converting.

If the Gentile partner happens to be a Christian, it's most likely that she or he will either (a) be expected to give up that faith, or (b) keep it as an entirely private matter that should not be regarded as a relevant topic for discussion within the Jewish community. That's because the idea that Jesus is the Messiah and Savior predicted in the Hebrew Scriptures is also seen as a threat to Jewish survival. So even when a Christian spouse is welcomed into the Jewish community, the couple will not be on equal footing when it comes to differences in religious identity. That makes it difficult to find spiritual harmony.

The idea that believing in Jesus is a threat to Jewish survival is so ingrained that it is actually seen as a basic element of Jewish identity. That is why a Jewish response to the gospel so often comes down to "That's fine for you but I'm Jewish." It is a "given" among Jewish people that Jesus is someone else's god, someone else's religion. That is why Mark (from the opening story in the introduction) pointed an angry finger at me and announced that he would never believe as I do.

A look at what the Bible says about intermarriage (see chapter 5) combined with a look at what it says about survival of the Jewish people reveals two things. Concern for Jewish survival does not require us to fight the tide of intermarriage. Concern for Jewish survival does not require us to close our hearts to the possibility that Jesus is our Messiah and Savior. My hope is that you'll find JGCs open to what the Bible says about Jewish survival, and that after a study, perhaps based on the material that follows, they will come to some helpful conclusions toward spiritual harmony.

A Biblical Hope for Jewry

God promised Abraham that He would preserve the Jewish people. They would exist as an enduring testimony to His name in the earth. The Lord promised to bless Abraham's name, to give him descendants with a land on which to settle as a nation and to call their home. Abraham's descendants were to be a sanctified people, set apart to serve the purposes of Yahweh. Thus, the policy against intermarriage was to protect them against foreign religious influence.

I'm confident that the survival of Jewish people has been in the hands of God from the start of time and creation. In Genesis 3:15, after the breach of relationship between God and human beings, we see the promise for reconciliation. That promise concerning "the seed of a woman" is the first in a long line of promises concerning the One who would remove the barrier of our offense and restore our relationship with God.

God called Abram and Sarah (see Genesis 12) to be the family through which He would bring into existence first the tribe, then the nation, through which that child of promise, the seed of a woman, could come into the world.

Abraham became the father of many nations. Among those nations would come one particular line of people and, from them, the child who would be a blessing to all the nations on the earth (Genesis 12:3). That anointed child would overcome the curse of alienation from God and accomplish all that was needed for reconciliation with God. So, He set apart the Jewish people to be the delivery system for the Messiah. Only through trusting in the grace work of that anointed servant could anyone be reconciled to God.

So then, are Jewish people just here to be a delivery system for the Messiah? Beyond that are Jewish people left to fend for their own survival, like some historical leftover?

Preservation of the Jewish people, beyond delivering the Messiah, had another purpose. God revealed Himself to the nations of the earth in that He is faithful to Israel and His Word is trustworthy in His promises. He made the people of Israel a testimony of His covenant-keeping character. If the Jewish people had a mission statement, it might read, "We exist to testify that God exists and keeps His promises. He is just, full of grace, loving and truthful. His character is demonstrated to all the nations in the way that He has kept His covenant relationship to our people."

Deuteronomy 7:6–9 provides God's rationale for choosing and preserving the Jewish people. Yahweh declared that He did not choose the people Israel because it was such a great and powerful nation. Israel was not a wealthy nation. It wasn't a massive people. If He wanted to select a big nation, He could have picked China, India or Assyria in its day. If He wanted a wealthy nation, He could have picked America. If He wanted a powerful empire, He could have picked Persia or Rome as His chosen people.

Instead He picked, according to His sovereign plan, a small and ordinary people around which He wrote biblical history. In doing so, He revealed His character in caring for Israel. All the kingdoms and nations of the earth could understand the power of God and His faithfulness in the way He safeguarded the survival of Jewish people. Through that little nation came the Lord's Messiah for all the nations. And yet, even in that role no single Israelite was guaranteed eternal life and salvation merely based on birthright. Each individual Israelite has to come to God, trusting and obeying Him in the same way that people from every other nation would come to know eternal life.

So first, Israel was called to be the delivery system for the Lord's anointed Savior-Messiah. Second the nation of Israel was set apart out of Abraham's seed to be a national testimony to Yahweh. Israel is preserved to demonstrate the Lord's character to all the nations of the earth. The hope for Jewish survival and preservation is insured upon the name and guarantee of God Himself.

Therefore, it's not necessary to focus on how to stop intermarriage. It is not the threat to the survival of the Jewish people. God will see to the continuation of world Jewry. We can trust Him for that.

And if (as we believe) the Jewish Bible points to Jesus as the promised Messiah, then embracing Him in no way lessens one's Jewish identity. In fact, following Jesus is one of the most satisfying ways a person can participate in God's promises concerning Jewish people and their destiny as a nation.

JGCs and especially the Jewish partner will commonly feel any combination of guilt, fear, or obligation associated with traditional Jewish views concerning intermarriage and/or Jesus as a threat to Jewish survival. Those feelings, in a Jewish community context, are even understandable. But they do not have to continue for those who examine them in a biblical context. In fact, JGCs will have a much better opportunity to find spiritual harmony without them.

Understanding God's promises and purposes for the survival of the Jewish people can relieve JGCs of unnecessary guilt and fear that they are threatening Jewish survival, either by intermarrying or by considering the claims of Jesus. God's promises and purposes for our survival also free us to examine what He has to say about redemption and whether Jesus is the Jewish Messiah.

Appendix 3: Intermarriage in the Bible

Common themes related to intermarriage unfold progressively throughout the Bible. You can use them in Bible study with a couple or in small group discussions—either as guides to further study or as possible discussion topics. Look for illustrative principles that might be useful to contemporary Jewish-Gentile couples.

Marriage among the Patriarchs: Abraham and Sons (Isaac, Esau and Jacob)
God made covenant promises to Abram. Abram believed God (Genesis 15:1–21), and the Lord Most High promised to give Abram's descendants a land as an everlasting possession. It was in that place that his descendants would live out God's covenant (Genesis 17:1–27). Abraham and his household were circumcised as a sign that he and subsequent parents were obedient to the covenant promises of God.

While in that land, God gave Abraham a son of promise, Isaac. When Abraham needed to seek a bride for his son Isaac, why did he send his servant back to Mesopotamia to find one? See Genesis 24:2–4. Was the reason racial, cultural or theological? There is a hint back in Genesis 15:16 and ahead in Deuteronomy 7:3.

A line of covenant promise emerged among the descendants of Abraham and Sarah. The concept of a remnant according to God's choosing surfaced as Jacob was part of the covenant people while his brother, Esau, was not—though he was a physical descendant of Abraham and Isaac.

Genesis 26:34–35 talks about Esau's choice when it came to marriage, and how it affected his parents. Who were the Hittites? Why were Esau's parents upset?

The first appearance of Israel's name occurred during Jacob's encounter with God in Genesis 32. The covenant was promised through Jacob and his family in Genesis 35:9–15. Jacob worshiped Yahweh, erecting an altar at Beth El to confirm his faith and his participation in the covenant promised to Abraham and his seed forever.

Marrying outside the Jewish people was not an issue for the patriarchs, since the Jewish people as a community with potential marriage partners did not exist until Jacob's children had children. Yet Abraham, Sarah, Isaac and Rebecca had definite ideas about which groups of people they did or didn't want their children to marry. The issue wasn't Jewish or not Jewish—so what was it?

Intermarriage before Sinai: Genesis 34:2
Dinah was a Jewish woman, the daughter of Leah and Jacob (Genesis 34). Shechem, a Canaanite, raped Dinah and then sought her hand in marriage by force. Simeon and Levi, sons of Jacob, avenged the rape of their sister by murdering Shechem and his friends and plundering their city. There was to be no marriage accommodation with the Canaanites.

Joseph, one of the tribal heads and son of Jacob, married Asenath, an Egyptian (Genesis 41:37–45). The Bible does not commend or condemn his choice.

Moses fled Pharaoh's house where he had been raised as a Egyptian, though he was a Hebrew. He spent the next 40 years among the Midianite people. These people were descendants of Abraham through another of his wives, Keturah. Moses took a Midianite wife named Zippora in Exodus 2:21. Apparently, through Moses she came to fear Yahweh. She circumcised their son according to the covenant God made with Abraham (Exodus 4:24–26).

Intermarriage Prohibition after Sinai: Exodus 34:14–16 and Deuteronomy 7:1–4
At Sinai, God instructed Moses to prohibit the Israelites from marrying the Canaanite people they would meet when He brought them into the Land of Promise. The issue was not racial, but one of spiritual character. The prohibition was to protect the Hebrews against the perverted religion and idolatrous influence of Canaanite nations (Exodus 34:10–17).

That should inform any concern that we have today about intermarriage. Those who believe in God are set apart to live differently from those who don't know God. They can and will endure harm to their faith through intimacy with people who do not share their love and faithfulness for the one true God.

Joshua to Judges: Intermarriage at the Conquest of Canaan
Joshua confirmed his loyalty to the Lord and his covenant with Abraham (see Joshua 24:1–28). He and the people recommitted to serving Yahweh prior to conquering the land of the Canaanites. They rejected any relationship with the Canaanites, their gods and their religious practices.

Joshua led by example, declaring, "As for me and my house, we will serve the LORD" (verse 15). He called the people to choose whom they would serve. In response to their affirming witness, Joshua says, "You are witnesses against yourselves that you have chosen the LORD for yourselves, to serve Him." They were to reject the people of that land and their foreign gods.

Shortly after that, Joshua led the assault on Jericho, while he spared Rahab, the Canaanite prostitute, and her family. He had respect for her faith in Yahweh, which prompted her to help the Israelites conquer Jericho. Her testimony of faith in Yahweh is found in Joshua 2:8–15. She told the Israelite spies what her people had heard about the powerful deeds of Yahweh. "And as soon as we heard these things, our hearts melted; neither did there remain any more courage in anyone because of you, for the LORD your God, He is God in heaven above and on earth beneath" (Joshua 2:11).

Rahab was a faithful remnant from among an enemy people, yet she became a follower of Yahweh and was welcomed into the Jewish nation. It is presumed that Rahab married into the Jewish people. She may well be the Rahab mentioned in Matthew 1:5 along with Ruth the Moabite—listed in the genealogy of Jesus.

In Judges 8, we hear of two Israelite "heroes" who were not completely faithful to Yahweh. Gideon defeated the Midianites. He was said to have had 70 sons, for he had "many wives." We do not know if those wives were from among the former people of the land, except for one who was "his concubine who was in Shechem [who] also bore him a son" (Judges 8:31).

During this period of time, Judges records Israel's history, saying, "As soon as Gideon was dead, . . . the children of Israel again played the harlot with the Baals, and made Baal-Berith their god. Thus the children of Israel did not remember the Lord their God, who had delivered them from the hands of all their enemies on every side" (Judges 8:33–34).

Samson's story is told in Judges 13–16. It is worth reading about this sad life of Samson, because it began with such promise. Samson was a gift and an answer to prayer for his father and mother from the tribe of Dan, who dedicated him as a Nazarite to God. Samson was set apart to deliver Israel from the Philistines (Judges 13:5).

Yet three times, Samson fell in love with and had relations with Philistine women. It is no surprise that they all turned his heart away from serving Yahweh. He ended his life as a captive of the Philistines. While imprisoned in Gaza and ridiculed as a trophy of their god Dagon, Samson finally called on the name of the Lord to destroy his captors and he died with them.

Ruth the Moabite: Ruth 1:1–4

The story of Ruth is also set during the time of the Judges and shows how God calls people from every nation (i.e., the Gentiles) to trust in Him. Ruth is among those Gentiles who were blessed through the covenant with Abraham in Genesis 12:1–3. She was a Moabite foreigner who had married a Jewish man. When her husband died, Ruth spoke of her loyalty to the God of the Israelites and her desire to remain with her mother-in-law, Naomi, and live within the Jewish community. God rewarded her humility and her loyalty to Him by giving her a husband, Boaz, and placing her in the honored line of the faithful. Her great-grandson was King David, and through her children came the Messiah Yeshua.

The Kings: Intermarriage in David and Solomon's Houses

Second Samuel 11 tells the shameful story of King David's covetousness of another man's wife. Bat Sheva (Bathsheba), a Jewish woman, was married to Uriah, a Hittite. This particular Hittite warrior from Anatolia became a loyal and valiant officer in King David's army. King David sacrificed his loyal servant Uriah in a murderous plot to cover up and further enable his adulterous relationship with Bat Sheva.

Ruth and Uriah are beloved in Israel, though they are always identified with their former Gentile nations. Still, they were fully integrated into the Jewish people. Their names are held in honor and blessing. Gentiles can, therefore, marry into the Jewish people without prejudice against their ethnicity and be welcomed and even honored according to their faith.

First Kings 11:1–5 describes the many foreign nations from which Solomon drew his wives. The same passage quotes Deuteronomy 7:3–4, which specifically repeats the prohibition against doing exactly what Solomon had done: "You shall not intermarry with them, nor they with you. Surely they will turn away your hearts after their gods."

Solomon married 700 wives and had 300 concubines; and his wives did turn his heart away from following the Lord. "His heart was not loyal to the LORD his God, as was the heart of his father David" (1 Kings 11:2–5). Solomon's example impacted his entire nation and the Jewish people paid a terrible price for centuries to come. The problem with intermarriage was not a matter of ethnicity but of being joined to idolatrous cultures.

Spiritual disunity can still destroy the faith of believers today, ruin marriages and interfere with the spiritual blessing of their children.

Exile and Return: Intermarriage in the Time of Esther, Ezra and Nehemiah
The book of Esther stands as a quiet testimony to Jewish faith that was rewarded in the midst of a very dark time in Israel's Diaspora history. Esther, of course, was a Jew married to the king of Persia, a Gentile. While the name of God is never mentioned in the book of Esther, it is very clear that God blessed Esther's faith and her example to her people. Yahweh was faithful for the sake of His covenant promise to the Jewish people. He honored Esther's courage to trust Yahweh while she was virtually a captive in the court of the Persian king. While she did not initiate and had little to say about her "intermarriage," God clearly used it for the preservation of the Jewish people.

Ezra 9 and 10; Nehemiah 13:23–27
The accounts of Ezra and Nehemiah describe the impact of intermarriage on the Jewish captives who'd been exiled in Persia. They returned to Jerusalem and the land of Judea in phases. During each of those returns, many of the priests (Cohanim) and elders of the people brought with them pagan wives they had married while in the lands of their captivity. The reports by these two historians at the end of the Babylonian captivity are filled with introspective agony about the spiritual harm that may be done to their people through these intermarriages.

Their generations had already experienced horrific judgment for spiritual infidelity. The people had seen the wrath of God and feared that it might once more come upon Israel. So sacrifices and guilt offerings were commanded. Any Jews who would not separate themselves from these intermarriages were treated harshly. The names of the offending priests were written in the book of Ezra to shame them. They were required to put away their spouses and held accountable for nearly bringing disaster upon the nation once again.

The book of Nehemiah is dated about 444 B.C. and documents the second returning population, approximately fourteen years after Ezra. Like Ezra, Nehemiah lived in the shadow of a horrific invasion and merciless deportation according to Yahweh's judgment for the nation's faithlessness. That faithlessness was the predicted outcome of marriage to pagan people.

Nehemiah posted guardians on the walls against those who would come against the city of Jerusalem. He called on God to guard His Jewish people against their own foolishness for intermarrying women of Ashdod, Ammon and Moab (Nehemiah 13:23).

In the verses that follow, Nehemiah described in the harshest terms the Jews who might lead Israel astray again in the same way King Solomon, king of Israel, sinned against Yahweh. Nehemiah did not bless Israel's spiritual leaders when he wrote, "Remember them, O my God, because they have defiled the priesthood and the covenant of the priesthood and the Levites." He was cleansing the nation for the spiritual good of his people.

Intertestament Times

When the Assyrians under King Sargon overran the northern kingdom, Jews were exiled into the lands of the Assyrians. Samaria, the region between Judea in the south and Galilee to the north, was repopulated with captives from other lands. The Samaritans intermarried with these Gentile deportees from conquered Assyrian territories.

Intermarriage between foreigners and Jews complicated the ancestry of these Samaritans. Returning Jews hated the Samaritans, considering them no longer pure racially or religiously.

This was the backdrop to the interaction between Jesus and the Samaritan woman in John 4:1–42. Jesus did not show prejudice against the Samaritans as other Jews had. In fact, the interaction with this Samaritan woman, recorded by John, contains one of the clearest statements of Jesus' Messianic claims. The woman said to him, "I know that Messiah is coming. . . . When He comes, He will tell us all things." Jesus said to her, "I who speak to you am He" (John 4:25–26).

Intermarriages in the New Testament: Timothy, Son of a Greek Father and a Messianic Jewish Mother

Timothy was the son of Eunice, a Jewish woman who had come to believe in Jesus. We're told a bit about her faith and practice of teaching the Scriptures to Timothy from his childhood (2 Timothy 3:15). We don't hear anything about his Gentile father who, it is supposed, was not a believer in Jesus. Yet Timothy is an important New Testament personality and a disciple of Paul. In fact, two New Testament books are written to Paul's "son in the faith" Timothy, who was the son of a Jewish-Gentile couple.

Admonition to Early Christians in 2 Corinthians 6:14 (See the context, 2 Corinthians 6:11–7:4)

This is where we see the phrase "unequally yoked." It refers back to Deuteronomy 22:10 which says, "You shall not plow with an ox and a donkey together." This proverb in Deuteronomy 22:9–11 told the Jewish people to be separate and distinct from the alien Canaanite nations and their ungodly spiritual influence.

Paul used this imagery of the unequal yoking of an ox and a donkey to describe the Corinthian Christians. He asked them to be different from the surrounding culture in Corinth, a sexually immoral and chaotic seacoast city. The Corinthian congregation of Jews and Gentiles had tolerated incest, fornication and drunkenness in the midst of their church congregation.

Paul asked the Corinthians to open their hearts to God and turn away from sinful entanglements. He told them to be single-minded and consistently faithful to Yahweh. They should separate themselves from the unholiness that was rampant in their city. He is saying, do not be any longer yoked to the culture of your community. Do not be unequally yoked as with a donkey and an ox.

Appendix 4: More Bible Study Topics for JGC Ministry

Following are suggested Bible studies topics that Jewish-Gentile couples might find relevant. Any one of these could become a focus for conversation with a Jewish-Gentile couple. You will notice an overlap with the previous appendix, which was given as a stand alone topic for a particular purpose.

Along with each topic, you'll find one or more Bible passages, and a summary thought to get you started. The first one gives examples of the kinds of study questions you can create to facilitate discussion and discovery. You might find one or more of these topics an appropriate opportunity for a Bible-based conversation, particularly when indicated by the questions couples ask or the challenges they describe.

Origins: God's Purpose for Marriage and Families

A. Man and Woman Created in God's Image and for His Purpose

Genesis 1:27–31

Because men and women are created in the image of God, we derive our worth, dignity and purpose from that glorious image.

Suggested study questions: What aspects of God's image has He imparted to humanity? How does that establish our worth? Is that different from the way people generally see one another? Are man and woman of equal worth based upon the way they were created? Was God pleased with His creation of man and woman?

God gave human beings incredible intrinsic worth by creating them in His image. He gave them authority to rule over His creation, earth, and all that is in it. In verse 28, He blessed them. And in verse 31, He said that everything that He had made was very good.

B. Sabbath Rest: Given for a Life of Trusting God

Genesis 1:31–2:3 and Hebrews 4:9–10

The concept of rest is usually connected with God having finished His work of creation. He rested in Himself and in His own sufficiency after seeing that everything He made was very good. Therefore, He asks all of humanity to do the same thing: that is, to rest in His sufficiency and to trust fully in Him. That is echoed in the New Testament, Hebrews 4:9–10. Sabbath is a day of worship, but it's more; it was given to teach us a way of life, daily trusting in God and His sufficient grace.

C. Marriage: The Biblical Perspective

Genesis 2:18–24

The creation story highlights the intimate interconnection between man and woman. They are created with the same worth and from the same flesh yet distinctly different in their complimentary physical composition. They are meant to fit together. He is *ish*, and she is *isha*, "man" and "woman."

The key phrase which frames marriage is found in Genesis 2:24. God envisioned the future composed of families where a father and a mother commit to a life together in a holy union for the purpose of creating children. When children marry, the man "shall leave his father and mother and be joined to his wife, and they shall become one flesh." That is God's design for marriage and society.

D. The Promise: Man and Woman Fallen and Relationship restored

Genesis 3:1–15

The free will God gave to human beings was a gift of love. It came with the possibility that people could choose against God, deciding not to trust Him. That is exactly what happened, and it explains the broken relationship between God and the people He created.

That choice not to trust God is the story of the fall. The consequences of that choice, that break in relationship, have infected every human being since. (See Romans 5:12–21.)

The key point in Genesis 3:15 is that God gave a promised solution to restore that relationship. He would send a male child, the seed of a woman, who would bruise or crush the head of the evil one while being bruised or wounded in the process. This is the seed of the woman who would be Immanuel, as described in Isaiah 7:14. That seed had to come from a specific woman and a family and a tribe and a nation. That history unfolds in the rest of the Bible. God would call a nation of people, the descendants of Israel, to be the chosen line through which He would bring redemption from sin. That nation would be the delivery system for the seed, the anointed Redeemer or Messiah, to reconcile Himself with all who believe. (See John 8:37–47.) He is Yeshua (Jesus), the child of promise. He is the seed who would die for the sin of the world and yet be resurrected, validating God's redemption of all sinners.

E. Grace: Banished from the Tree of Life (Etz Chaim) as an Act of Love

Genesis 3:16–24

Adam and Eve were separate from God. Their relationship had been broken through their dishonor to His trustworthiness. If they had additionally eaten from the Tree of Life, they would have been permanently sealed into that broken, fallen and separated state. God in His grace put them out of the garden and posted guards to save them from that terrible fate. Their expulsion from the garden was God's will as an act of love, not an act of punishment or hatred toward Adam and Eve or humanity.

F. Family Life: Even under the Curse

Genesis 4

Sex is a gift from God. Sexual relations between a man and a woman in marriage are considered holy and are for pleasure and producing children. However, from the very beginning, sin has affected every human relationship.

God holds people accountable for the outworking of sin. What happened to Cain as a result of his killing Abel? Verse 16 says that the Lord sent him away from His presence. The last two verses summarize the lineage from Adam down to Enosh. The latter was to be the link in a line of promise down to Noah. In that time people were preaching and witnessing and testifying about the name of the Lord. They knew Him and His reputation as a God of grace. Some people understood His loving, gracious nature and His promise to redeem all sinners from the curse of sin.

As in Bible times, people are still accountable to God when our acts of self-interest and faithlessness hurt others. Very often though, people don't realize that failure to treat one another with grace and dignity stems from a failure to recognize our disconnect from God. That carries with it a lack of understanding of how He intended us to live as people who bear His image.

Origins: Jews and Gentiles

A. Remnants: The Salvation of the Nations in Noah

Genesis 6–8:22

In His patience, God allows nations to multiply, and with them the practice and influence of sin in society—but only to a point. The evil that people are doing to themselves and to one another has to be judged. Genesis 6:8 introduces the idea that through Noah, God would save a remnant of humanity apart from all the nations. The rest of this chapter shows how God lavished grace upon those who trusted Him. The section concludes in 8:20 with Noah worshiping God in response to His salvation and blessing.

B. God's Covenant: Covenant with the Nations, the Goyim

Genesis 9:1–19

This section opens with the recommissioning and affirmation of God's purpose for humanity to be fruitful and multiply and fill the earth. God gives a sign of covenant promise in the rainbow. He promises never again to judge humanity with a flood that wipes out all the nations save one. The basis for all nations that would follow comes from the sons of Noah: Shem, Ham and Japheth.

C. Nations Scattered: The Origin of Abram

Genesis 11

The post-flood nations join to build a tower to heaven; the implication is their determination to rule themselves by self-reliance and self-sufficiency. Again, God in His grace judges that effort to circumvent His sovereignty. He confuses the nations and scatters them from that place as an expression of His grace. God knows the evil that will result from a humanity united in purpose with one another, yet at odds with God and His rightful rule.

Humanity was created to love and trust God, and it is His intent to redeem the human race for that purpose. Chapter 11 concludes with an introduction of the family of Abram. Yahweh would call him to leave his homeland and become the forefather of nations—including the nation of Israel through whom the seed of the woman in Genesis 3:15 would finally come to accomplish that redemption.

D. The Jews: God's Covenant Plan through His Chosen People

Genesis 12

God's covenant with Abraham includes three great provisions: he will be made a great nation, his name will be blessed, and all the nations of the earth will be blessed through him.

That covenant with Abraham was a unilateral covenant, signed by God alone with the promise guaranteed by His name and character and not reliant on the actions of Abraham or the Jews. In fact the only thing that Abraham contributed to signing the covenant was that "He believed in the LORD, and He accounted it to him for righteousness" (Genesis 15:6).

From among the Jews would come the tribe of Judah, King David, and eventually the person of Messiah Yeshua, Jesus. Though Jesus came to and through the Jewish people, His salvation would be for people of all nations, to whomever would receive Him—so fulfilling the promise of all nations being blessed through Abraham.

Though the covenant with Abraham promised a blessing to all the nations, that salvation was only realized in the lives of those who would receive Him: in a sense, a chosen remnant. In the same way, salvation would come to a remnant of the Jewish people—to those who receive it through Jesus.

Appendix 5: Stumbling Blocks and Challenges

If you are seasoned in ministry to Jewish people you've already navigated through these stumbling blocks and challenges and you'll probably want to skim through this appendix. But if you are less experienced, I know from training new mission workers and Christian volunteers that even after completing this workbook, you might still lack the confidence of a Navy SEAL. This appendix can help build your confidence. So, let's think through some of the stumbling blocks and pitfalls that you might encounter as you present the good news of Messiah Jesus to Jewish people. Understanding them better will help smooth your path.

You Think I'm Going to Hell?!

You've already seen throughout this workbook that most Jewish people are not personally concerned with hell, as it does not fit in with normative Jewish teaching about afterlife. So how is it that a Jewish partner can so easily become angry over their partner's concern that, without Jesus, they are going to hell—which in the minds of most, doesn't even exist?

Here's another case study that we can analyze to get to the answer to that, as well as suggestions for an approach that could encourage a less volatile response.

A Christian, Marcia, told her Jewish boyfriend, "Eric," of her concern that he wouldn't go to heaven with her. She knew that he loved her, but she could also tell that heaven or hell really didn't matter to him. He thought about her anxiety for a few moments when a cloud of resentment gathered across his normally cheery face.

"Wait a minute," he abruptly said. "You think I'm going to hell?! Really? You think I'm going to hell because I don't believe in Jesus?!"

Marcia went pale. She felt that she had said something terribly wrong. She was trying to tell Eric how much she cared for him. He couldn't see that at all. He was angry and offended. What can we learn from this exchange?

Marcia believes heaven is real from reading the Bible. She also assumed that Eric had a complete grasp of the Hebrew Scriptures (aka "Old Testament") just because he is Jewish. Those Scriptures don't talk extensively about an afterlife, but they do talk about eternity and mention life after death. So, Marcia assumed that Eric must have a belief in heaven like hers. Nope!

Questions are the best preventative when it comes to assumptions. Marcia could have approached the subject by asking Eric just what he thought about "heaven." She could follow that up by asking, "How do you know that is true?" Or she could have listened patiently and then let him know that she understands the idea of heaven in a way that is different from him. One sensitive question could have warded off a cross-cultural collision.

In the beginning of their conversation she also could have asked his permission: "Is it okay if we talk about life after death? I'm curious what you believe." Getting an okay to go into a sensitive topic goes a long way to prevent a person from feeling presumed upon.

What about Eric's "question": "You think I'm going to hell because I don't believe in Jesus?!" His angry question was also an accusation, probably intended to end the discussion—and that's exactly what happened.

So, how can you respond to this question, and/or teach others to do so? While simply saying yes is a genuine response, it doesn't open communication with the other person. Try a Jewish cultural response: answer a question with a question!

Eric: "Do you think I'm going to hell because I don't believe in Jesus?!"
Marcia: "Eric, do you really believe that there is a place called 'hell?'"
Eric: "No, not really."
Marcia: "Then why make an issue of it with me if you don't think it matters?"

This is not a deep exchange, but it might open the door for a deeper exchange later. Eric may or may not be able to articulate why he made an issue of it. Although he does not believe much if anything about an afterlife, he is still conditioned to think of it in a certain way by popular culture. That informs his own assumptions about anyone who believes he is not going to heaven. For example:

1. Heaven is supposed to be for good people, so if you think I have to believe like you do to get there, you must think you are better than I am.

2. If you believe in heaven, you probably also believe in hell. Hell is supposed to be for bad people, so if you think I'm going there, you are judging me unfairly.

Over and over you see fantasy movies that lightheartedly depict heaven as a place of reward for being good. Often those who haven't been quite good enough to enter are given tasks to do back on earth so that they can earn their way through the pearly gates.

While people know these movies are fictional, they stem from and propagate a certain perspective that measures everything in terms of what we can do or what we can deserve. Heaven is depicted as a good place for good people, but rarely is it shown to be the place that is full of God's presence and glory.

If you have permission to state your own contrasting views about the afterlife, the perspective can shift dramatically.

The biblical view is that heaven is the outcome of a relationship with God that begins by receiving His offer of reconciliation here on earth. It's fair to ask any person who has little interest in that relationship if or why they would expect to find that their eternal destiny is to enjoy that relationship forever. In the same way, if hell is eternal separation from God, it's fair to ask why anyone who is content to live as though God either doesn't exist or is not worth knowing would be surprised to find that the already existing separation from God has been made permanent. Again, both heaven and hell are not about religion, but about a relationship—or lack of relationship—with God.

There is another way to respond to an accusation like Eric's, which wrongly assumes that we think not believing in Jesus causes people to go to hell. According to the Bible, people go to hell because of sin, not "because of Jesus." It's important to point out the distinction. Just remember from our earlier chapters that sin is not an especially meaningful word to people who are not biblically oriented.

Angry Responses (General)

Angry responses are not restricted to conversations about an afterlife. Any number of topics might hit a nerve, that is, be perceived as a threat to a core value. If you say or ask something that is perceived as a threat to Jewish survival or even personal Jewish identity, you (or the Gentile partner in a JGC) might inadvertently trip a spiritual land mine.

Sometimes an angry reaction is an indication that someone has begun to consider what you are saying. Anger is one way to respond when a person recognizes change is a possibility if they continue moving in that direction. Anger can also indicate their awareness that God might ask things that they are not ready to give or to do. On one hand, He respects our will, asking us to simply open a door and welcome Him in. On the other hand, He is the sovereign of the universe meaning He has all the power. Anyone that huge is likely to be a little scary. He could come into your life and change a lot of things! That can feel discomforting, sometimes depressing or frightening, and may not be welcomed. You are merely God's instrument to present His loving message. Anger is a natural reaction from a selfish heart that doesn't want to give up control to anyone. But the very fact that a person reacts can be more encouraging than someone who simply ignores or does not care about the message.

So how do you respond?

The wisdom of Proverbs 15:1 applies: "A soft answer turns away wrath." Sometimes the "soft answer" is a gentle question.

When things get tense, I sometimes try asking, "Forgive me for asking, but do you know what is making you angry right now?" A little bit of thoughtful introspection can give the person relief in an emotional "timeout."

Sometimes that anger is actually frustration. When people sense that God is good and loving, often they recognize there's something wrong inside of them that they don't know how to fix. I trust God enough to take a cautious, slow approach, and encourage them to give God time to work in their life. He is the one who prepares their sense of understanding to hunger after truth. In my experience, until they ask for the answer to the dilemma: "There is something wrong in me, and I don't know how to fix it," let God prepare their heart for the right moment. When they ask, they are ready for truth that changes everything.

So remember, sometimes an angry reaction indicates that you've touched a spiritual nerve. It can also indicate that truth is breaking through. It doesn't necessarily mean that you've done anything wrong. An angry reaction is not necessarily a red light to further conversation. It must be met with caution and gentleness.

You have probably heard it said, but when you can't talk with your Jewish friend (or anybody) about Jesus, back off for a period and speak with Jesus about your friend.

Terrible Crimes against Jewish People in the Name of Jesus

A common stumbling block exists on account of many awful things that have been done to Jewish people in the name of Jesus. Let reason push that stumbling block aside. Is unreasonable to assume that the same God who blessed the descendants of Abraham would perpetrate acts of hatred on them through Crusaders, Inquisitors, or nationalist anti-Semites? And is it reasonable that the same Jesus who wept over Jerusalem and described Himself as the Good Shepherd who came to seek and to save the lost would encourage His followers to murder in His name? One has only to read the Sermon on the Mount or the prayer Jesus taught His disciples to say to realize that acts of hatred and cruelty are in stark contrast to everything Jesus stood for.

Horrible acts are often perpetrated in the name of a noble cause because very few people are able or willing to admit that their acts are evil. Attempts to connect themselves to a just or noble cause can misrepresent the cause but cannot change the character of the cause. So atrocities allegedly done in the name of the gospel can never nullify its truth. The Savior didn't come to judge, but to save (John 12:47).

Fear That Discussing Some Topics Will Result in a Hurtful Exchange

One of the top five challenges Jewish-Gentile couples reported was difficulty in understanding one another's religious differences. The inability to discuss those differences with any satisfying outcome often produced hurt feelings and a sense of alienation—more so between married couples. Partners expressed hesitation or fears about reopening such conversations because they could easily become heated.

Fear of damaging their relationship is understandable, but unfortunately it has hindered couples from finding spiritual harmony. Difficult discussions are necessary in order to work through challenges—otherwise they wouldn't be challenges! But you can help create understanding by gently and thoughtfully engaging discussions about religious beliefs, using the skills you have learned in previous chapters. Entering these discussions with both partners' consent and staying the course with sensitivity is one way to serve them. Encourage them not to give up and express confidence that with patience, they will be able to move into a place of understanding one another's differences.

If I Believe, I Won't Be Jewish

I was about ten when my Hebrew teacher told our bar-mitzvah preparatory class, "Jesus was Jewish until he converted to Christianity and then he wasn't Jewish anymore." That set an obstacle in the way of any path that we might take that could lead to Jesus. Jewish survival, we were told, is inconsistent with following Jesus.

How can we get around that stumbling block? For one thing, remember that Jewish identity is not predicated on the Jewish religion. There are many Jews who are agnostic or even atheist. But in addition to that, it is extraordinarily helpful to remember that the gospel of Jesus is not a religion. It's good news about a transforming relationship with God. The history of the Jewish people throughout our Bible focuses on relationships between people and the God of Abraham, Isaac and Jacob. Relationship with God is in contrast to following a religion. If this point isn't clear to you, I can commend a one-page summary in Tim Keller's book *Center Church* (Zondervan, 2012). See "A Quick Comparison of Religion and the Gospel" on page 65.

Begin a conversation with someone who is Jewish starting with your religion, the New Testament, or Jesus, and you will often just set off the Jewish survival reaction. Be patient. Be transparent. Ask questions that help you know where the other person is coming from spiritually. Finally, when you talk about God, it should be apparent that you are talking about someone who matters to you, someone who has proven trustworthy in your life. Your relationship with Him isn't about your particular culture or ethnicity; it's about the God who created diversity and transcends every culture. Yet this is also the God who chose the Jews to bring forth His revelation and redemption to all people, and to stand as a testimony to His faithfulness.

Theological

Many if not most objections Jewish people raise to the gospel have to do with the perception of who we are and what we must do or not do to remain Jews. Occasionally you will hear a theological objection. Sometimes even these are a smokescreen for an underlying concern about Jewish identity and survival, but not always.

A familiar objection is, "Jews only believe in one God—not three (like the Christians)." A statement like that is telling you, "I can't believe as you do because I'm a monotheist and you're not." It's a good idea to refocus on who God is rather than who we are. Certainly God tells us that He is one God, and there are no other gods beside Him. However, God does not explain Himself or His infinite nature. He doesn't seem to expect us finite beings to fully comprehend Him.

The Scriptures do hint that our one God is complicated. We read about the Spirit of God, we see some Hebrew constructs regarding God that are plural, such as "Let Us make man in Our image." The words of the Scripture on which we base our faith in one God is Deuteronomy 6:4: "Hear, O

Israel: The Lord our God, the Lord is one!" The word for *one* is not the simplest word for a singular one; rather it is the same word used to describe a unity, as in Genesis 2:24, where the man and wife "become one flesh."

We even have a mysterious verse in the book of Proverbs: "Who has ascended into heaven, or descended? Who has gathered the wind in His fists? Who has bound the waters in a garment? Who has established all the ends of the earth? What is His name, and what is His Son's name, if you know?" (Proverbs 30:4).

We can safely affirm that there is only one God, while acknowledging that He speaks both of His Spirit and His Son.

I have an observant friend who insisted, "God would never appear in the form of a man." I responded in a culturally appropriate manner with a logical question! "Is there anything that God can't do?" Benjamin was a judge, so he has an open mind about legitimate evidence. He conceded that God could do anything that is consistent with His nature. Omnipotence is part of His sovereignty. However, he wanted support from our Hebrew Scriptures.

With his consent, we looked at Genesis 32:22–32 in his own Hebrew Bible. Benjamin insisted the account of Jacob's wrestling match at Peniel was about Jacob and "an angel." Even the rabbis' superscript in his Bible depicted the event as Jacob "wrestling with an angel." I asked, "What if the Hebrew text tells a different story?" He was willing to let the text speak for itself.

Genesis 32:24 reads, "Then Jacob was left alone; and a Man wrestled with him until the breaking of day." First, Jacob's wrestling opponent was a man. Even the Hebrew text does not describe him as a messenger or as an angel. In fact, the only reference to a "messenger/angel" was in the rabbinic commentary on the page margin of Benjamin's Bible.

Second, the texts said that the unnamed wrestler prevails over Jacob and gives Jacob a new name, "Israel" ("one who struggles with God"). The wrestler subdued Jacob and then blessed him in that place. There was muscle versus muscle in that wrestling match. It was a manly contest.

Last, the text says that Jacob was so changed by the encounter that he memorialized the place, calling it Peniel with this explanation: "For I have seen God face to face, and my life is preserved" (Genesis 32:30). The text said Jacob actually recognized that he had grappled with God even "face to face."

The text convinced my friend Benjamin that he had been taught inaccurately by the rabbis. Indeed, God had appeared in human form as reported in the Torah. Benjamin was able to see that God could and actually did appear in human form elsewhere in the Hebrew Scriptures. The Lord can open human hearts if we present and allow the text of Scripture to speak.

Appendix 5

Resources

I've written a blog for EvangelVision.com titled "Why Is It So Hard to Talk to Jewish People about Jesus?" You can find it here: http://www.evangelvision.com/why-is-it-so-hard-for-jewish-people-to-hear-about-jesus/.

I've also written a series of articles that address these and other issues. You can find them at Gospel-Life.net, in partnership with the Billy Graham Center for Evangelism at Wheaton College. http://www.gospel-life.net/?s=jewish+people

Why Bother Jewish People with the Gospel of Messiah Jesus?
Posted by Billy Graham Center for Evangelism | On 13 December 2013

Why Is It So Hard for Jewish People to Hear the Gospel?
Posted by Billy Graham Center for Evangelism | On 21 March 2014

Why Can't They Hear What I'm Saying?
Posted by Billy Graham Center for Evangelism | On 4 July 2014

Patience & Evangelism: A Galatians 5:22–3 Series
Posted by Billy Graham Center for Evangelism | On 17 October 2014

What Are You Saying?? It's Like Speaking a Different Language
Posted by Billy Graham Center for Evangelism | On 14 January 2015

Let the Text Speak for Itself
Posted by Billy Graham Center for Evangelism | On 23 April 2015

"I Was Just 'Jewish Stupid'": Why Words Really Are Important in Gospel Communications
Posted by Billy Graham Center for Evangelism | On 31 July 2015

Addressing the Jewish Identity in Gospel Witness
Posted by Billy Graham Center for Evangelism | On 6 October 2015

Trust as the Foundation for Jewish Faith in Jesus
Posted by Billy Graham Center for Evangelism | On 8 October 2015

Appendix 6: The Engels Scale

I have found this chart to be helpful as I consider where people I minister to are at spiritually. You might find it useful to look at this scale and think back to your own faith journey. Remember how becoming a disciple of Jesus was, and continues to be, a process.

The Engels Scale

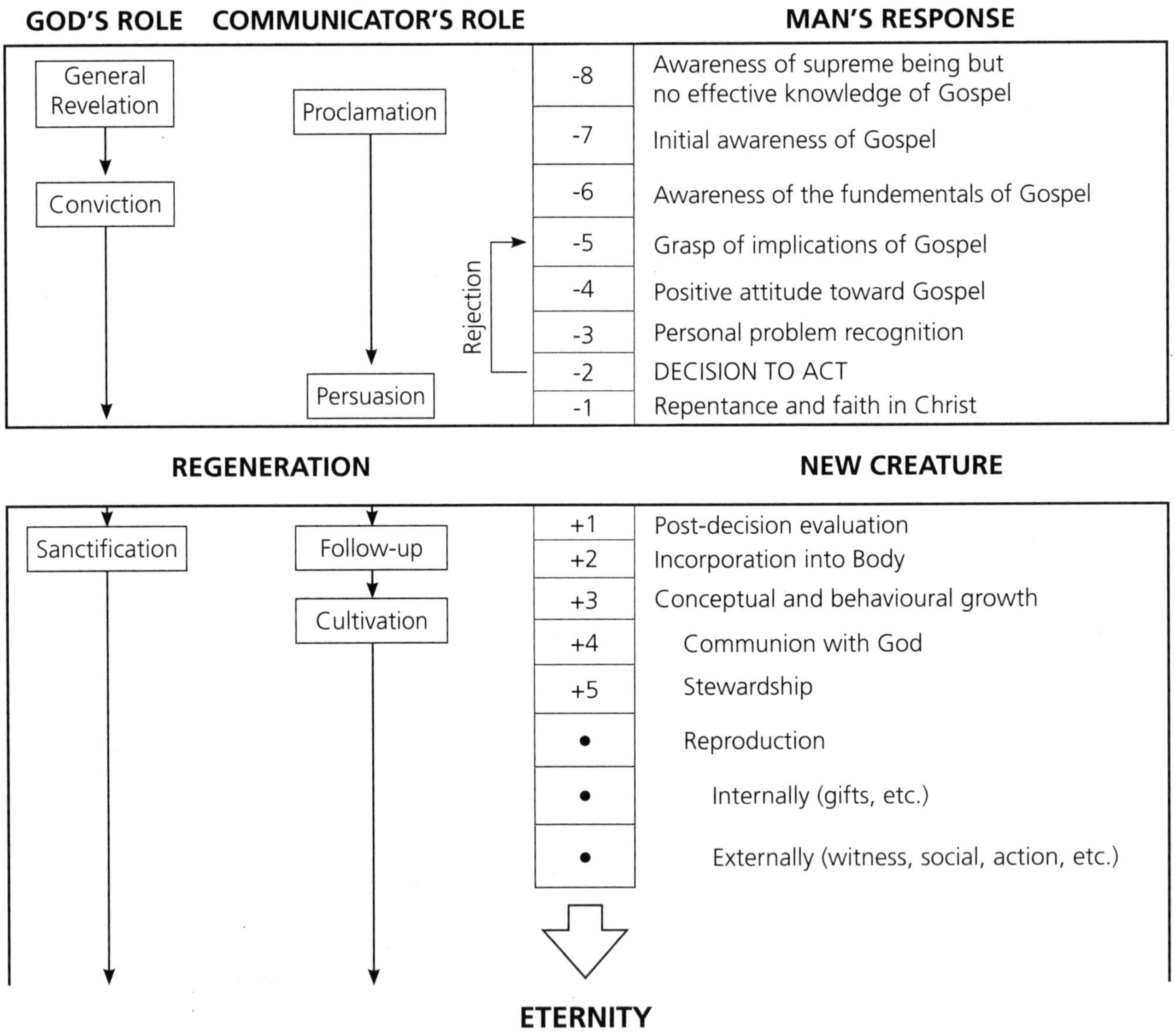

"Engles Scale of Evangelism" from *What's Gone Wrong With the Harvest?* by James F. Engel and Wilbert Norton (Grand Rapids: Zondervan, 1975), 67–68.

Appendix 7: More about Life-Cycle Events

December Holidays

December is a special month because Hanukkah/Christmas occur in the same season and are often seen as being in tension if not competition with one another. That's why Jewish-Gentile couples sometimes refer to the "December Dilemma."

Jewish-Gentile couples have to navigate through the wide array of symbols, meanings and traditions of Hanukkah and Christmas. The season is dominated by traditions or secular culture mixed with religious displays, trees and manger scenes. The Jewish community views Hanukkah as a season to relive the power of Jewish survival, telling the story of the Maccabees. Every colored light and even the particular holiday greeting can signal the "dominant" (non-Jewish culture) versus a Jewish minority.

That season can be a fantastic opportunity for ministry. However, it has to be approached with sensitivity to the diversity of cultures and awareness of what it might feel like to be a minority culture within a dominant culture. And it's not only Jews who are cultural outsiders at this time. I actually feel evangelical Christians are as well, because the dominant American culture and tradition in December is very secular. The birth of Messiah Jesus is easily overshadowed by a deluded, unbiblical feel-good season fed by movies and seasonal songs about snow, elves, Santa, or even peace and goodwill to men that leaves God completely out of the picture.

Yet December also can be a time for us to help Jewish-Gentile couples connect with the genuine meanings of the holidays. Hanukkah is a celebration of Jewish survival. Christmas is the story of the Messiah's birth. We can have a wonderful opportunity to communicate those messages cross-culturally.

Of course these celebrations are much less complicated if the couple shares a belief in Jesus as the Jewish Messiah. But even if they don't, there should be room for both couples to observe traditions that are important to each in a way that does not make one another feel put-upon. Sensitivity to one another's cultural identity is key.

Jewish-Gentile Weddings

If you take a moment to look back at the chart in chapter 4, you'll discover some unique cross-cultural challenges in the quadrant Wedding Event: Life-Cycle Issues.

Some couples told me how they avoided discussing their upcoming wedding, because they didn't want to introduce stress into their relationship. Of course that only postpones the stress, which intensifies as the date draws nearer. A wedding ceremony is a significant rite of passage and a Jewish-Gentile wedding ceremony can be a blessed time for spiritual ministry. However, the plans can involve a lot of negotiating and navigating between the cultures involved when bringing a

Jewish-Gentile couple together. Cultural land mines abound, and if you are involved in planning, you need to consult both families to identify and defuse those land mines.

The wedding ceremony should reflect the convictions of the couple. Premarital conversations can provide wonderful opportunities for ministry to the partners. Officiating clergy owes it to the couple to explain their own spiritual convictions about marriage. For example, in keeping with the doctrinal statement of my own ordination, I would not officiate a wedding where one person was a believer in Jesus and the other was not. In such a situation, I am glad to provide premarital counseling. However, early on in the conversation I would honestly tell them, "I am probably not the person to do your wedding ceremony." I don't want them to feel that my position is a judgment on them. I explain that my views of the Bible and Messiah Jesus require me to speak of both when I explain the meaning of marriage. If that testimony is not comfortable for them, I would excuse myself so as not to cause them embarrassment in front of their families. I wouldn't want to ruin a beautiful opportunity for ministry at a later time.

There are far too many potential cultural pitfalls to explore in a simple workbook like this. If you are helping to plan a Jewish-Gentile wedding you can avoid many of them simply by seeking advice and taking note of as many cultural signals as you can (see chapter 7). For example, on which side of the groom will the bride stand? The answer will involve some cultural expectations. Standing on the groom's left side signals that it is a Gentile or Christian wedding. If she stands at his right hand, it is a Jewish wedding. In some situations it won't matter. You would be surprised at how uncomfortable people can get when the slightest cultural expectation is overlooked.

One woman, a lawyer from a Greek Orthodox family, told me about her efforts to plan a wedding ceremony with her Jewish fiancé. His ideas about what a wedding should be were very different than hers. His expectations, and those of his family, were based on Jewish traditions. The couple had to constantly negotiate through their different culture symbols throughout their wedding plans.

She told me that in planning their wedding, "It never occurred to me that he was Jewish." She discovered this when he casually told her that he really didn't care about the wedding ceremony, but his parents might be uncomfortable if there were any Christian elements in the service. They worked out one compromise. They agreed that any time the name Jesus was going to be said in a prayer or the liturgy during the Greek Orthodox Christian wedding ceremony, her priest would say His name in the Greek language! The family understood that Jesus would be mentioned, but as long as they didn't have to hear or recognize His name, they were all right with it.

In another case, Henry, the son of Holocaust survivors, described why he and Mary needed to have two wedding ceremonies. Her family is Catholic, so they had a Catholic wedding. Henry's parents didn't object until they saw their Jewish son bowing before the Catholic priest to receive a blessing on their marriage. Afterwards they insisted that Henry and Mary also be married by a rabbi, just to make sure it was kosher.

Couples can become so overwhelmed by the daunting trial of clearing cross-cultural hurdles that they resign themselves to not having a ceremony. In my opinion, they miss a wonderful opportunity for celebrating an important life transition simply to avoid dealing with tensions that will surface again in the future anyway. The Elvis Wedding Chapel in Las Vegas is not a rockin' alternative! A wedding ceremony is just the first of many life-cycle events that a Jewish-Gentile couple will have to navigate. There will always be questions to ask each of the partners about what various cultural symbols mean. Explaining each symbol is only the beginning of the communication process. Next, the discussion leads to a decision about whether to choose one or the other cultural symbol or if there will be a blending of symbols. I will always remember a wedding ceremony that demonstrated some very thorough thinking about cultural symbols.

It was a wedding ceremony for two young doctors. One was from a conservative Jewish background and the other from a Chinese Baptist family. Co-officiating the ceremony were the groom's father, a rabbi, and the bride's father, a Baptist pastor. The ceremony included traditional symbols from both cultures and liturgical selections in Hebrew and in Chinese languages. Every cultural element had to be negotiated and then navigated carefully with great forethought. The couple was able to express their Christian faith, while delicately embracing family cultural preferences and the cultural comfort of guests. It was a pretty tricky feat, but great care was taken and the result of the time and thoughtfulness invested in the plans was a beautiful and meaningful cross-cultural event.

You can serve a Jewish-Gentile couple by helping them explore as many of their cultural signals as possible. They may discover deeper meanings through the process. These kinds of conversations might not necessarily create the path to finding spiritual harmony. However, the process can reveal or illustrate the need for that harmony. Weddings and many of the other life-cycle events offer opportunities for spiritual ministry to JGCs.

The following terminology and questions might be useful if you are helping couples discuss various cultural signals:

Officiate: Will there be a pastor, minister, priest, rabbi, one officiate or co-officiates?

Bride Position: In a Jewish wedding, the bride is on the right hand of the groom. In a non-Jewish wedding, she stands on the groom's left hand.

Culture Signals/Symbols: A wedding canopy or chuppah is an obvious Jewish symbol. So is a Magen David or Star of David. The obvious Christian symbol is that of a cross or a Bible. A Jewish symbol also might be the two tablets of Moses that symbolize the Torah. Would a couple use both, or neither and have a secular statement to their wedding ceremony?

Readings: Poems, secular romantic writing, or will there be Bible readings, including Ruth 1:16, Proverbs 31 or the "love is" chapter in 1 Corinthians 13?

Prayers: Will they use the Lord's Prayer or perhaps the seven Hebrew benedictions from the Jewish liturgy?

A Cup: Will the couple use a communion cup or will there be a kiddush cup to sanctify the marriage?

Candles: Will there be a seven-branched menorah or a unity candle?

Music: Will there be chanted Hebrew liturgical songs like "L'Echa Dodi" or Christian songs or secular love songs?

Liturgy: Will there be a Christian liturgy or a liturgy from Jewish tradition with Hebrew language?

Location: Church, synagogue, public venue like a park, private wedding hall, a home, or will there be two separate services to represent traditions of Judaism and Christian belief?

Dancing: Will there be traditional Jewish dances, secular dancing, a combination of both, or no dancing?

Circumcision

God gave circumcision as the sign of His covenant with Abraham. Circumcision of a Jewish baby boy is an appropriate cultural rite of passage that demonstrates the faith of the parents (since the child is only a passive participant). The parents are recognizing the covenant that God made with Abraham and its application to their child. The ceremony can be done at a hospital or at home. It can be performed with a symbolic prick of the heel at home after a hospital physician has done the actual circumcision cut. In my view, it doesn't need to be done by a rabbi or a Jewish clergy who is trained in the practice (a *mohel*). The important feature is that the family and community are gathered to honor the parents' affirmation and to observe that this child is identified within the line of Abraham, Isaac and Jacob. Our Jews for Jesus Ministry can help you find people to officiate at these rites of passage.

Hospital Visits

Not all life-cycle events are so joyous as a wedding or *bris* (circumcision). The less joyous the occasion, the fewer people will tend to "be there" for those who are undergoing the event. That is why visits to a hospital can provide an important service to those who are sick and dying and also to their family members. These visits can build relationships through demonstrating genuine care. Few of us find hospitals a pleasant environment, which is why a personal visit to a sick friend is more valuable than sending a "get well" card. I was trained to keep hospital visits short, only between 15 and 20 minutes. If I'm invited by the family to stay longer, I might stay as long as 30–40 minutes. Take time to pray for the person in the hospital bed, and for the family if they welcome it. Try to become familiar and sensitive about any particular cultural expectations. A professional hospital chaplain can be of help in this regard.

Funerals

Funerals are especially important rites of passage that can minister to Jewish-Gentile couples and their families. Just attending a funeral expresses great care to a family. Times for socializing after the funeral ceremony can be particularly unique. You can find a few rituals associated with a Jewish funeral by using an online resource. The most important service you can render is just being present with and for family members at their time of grief.

Conversations after a funeral can be significant and spiritually fruitful. It isn't necessary and may not be helpful to initiate conversations at that time. If you're a known and trusted friend, you may find Jewish people asking you some serious spiritual questions. That's often because little of what is said in a traditional Jewish funeral gives any hope of eternal life.

Rabbi Shaman Kanter said just two decades ago, "God is the last subject that can cause embarrassment in polite social conversation among Jewish people today, as once did discussion of death, sex or cancer."[1]

What word of Scripture is appropriate by which you can encourage people at a traditional Jewish funeral? Reference to the resurrection hope in Jesus might not be welcome unless the person who died was a Jewish believer in Jesus.

Few Jewish people other than the very orthodox have a concept of resurrection. I commend the writings of Job as most appropriate for speaking about resurrection at a Jewish funeral. He was a Gentile contemporary of Abraham who wrote amazing wisdom literature. In Job 19:23–27 he wrote,

> Oh, that my words were written!
> Oh, that they were inscribed in a book!
> That they were engraved on a rock
> With an iron pen and lead, forever!
> For I know that my Redeemer lives,
> And He shall stand at last on the earth;
> And after my skin is destroyed, this I know,
> That in my flesh I shall see God,
> Whom I shall see for myself,
> And my eyes shall behold, and not another.
> How my heart yearns within me!
> (Job 19:23–27)

---

1. Siammai Kanter "They're Playing Our Song," in *Moment*. 9/3 (March 1984): 38.

References for Further Reading

Parker, David, ed. *Jesus, Salvation and the Jewish People: The Uniqueness of Jesus and Jewish Evangelism*. London: Paternoster Press, 2011.

Rosen, Ceil and Moishe. *Witnessing to Jews: Practical Ways to Relate the Love of Jesus*. San Francisco: Purple Pomegranate Productions, 1998. A sample chapter is available online at http://www.jewsforjesus.org/files/pdf/other/wtj_sample.pdf.

Zaretsky, Tuvya, ed. Lausanne Occasional Paper 60: "Jewish Evangelism—A Call to the Church," 2004, http://www.lausanne.org/wp-content/uploads/2007/06/LOP60_IG31.pdf.

Acknowledgments

First I want to thank my wife and soul mate, Ellen Zaretsky, for typing every single word of this manuscript. She was the first line of correction and edits. I thank God that we are privileged to share life and our ministry to so many Jewish-Gentile couples. We are blessed to participate in this incredible spiritual journey together.

I appreciate the enormous work of Ruth Rosen in editing this manuscript. Ruth, thank you for helping me find the voice to say stuff in a less boring style. Our readers have been helped by your effort as editorial translator. You deserve some credit for making more understandable what I was really trying to communicate in many places. Thanks to Alicia Murphy for her patience and care in the time consuming and not-so-exciting but very necessary task of making proofreading corrections.

Grateful acknowledgement goes to Donald K. Smith, Enoch Wan, Mikel Neumann and Mary Wilder at Western Seminary. Your tireless effort helped shape the research and perspectives behind this project. You taught me the meaning of "culture" and where to find the missiological bridge to reach people from within one to another cultural perspective.

Thank you, David Brickner, for encouraging this project and Susan Perlman for pulling the pieces together. Marc Sternberg, I'm grateful for your wisdom and idea for the title. David Yapp and Paige Saunders, we are blessed by your pictorial cultural contributions in the cover art and layout. Likewise, appreciation to my ministry colleagues, Susan Montroy and Deni Hase. Susan spent a chunk of her life transcribing research interviews, papers and sections of my dissertation. Deni had the vision of this project and cheered the value of the ministry in it for more than two decades.

Thanks to the many Jewish-Gentile couples who have taught me so much. I especially want to mention Stacey Katz and Daryl McKillion along with Susan Curson and our brother Mark Resnick, who awaits us in the presence of Messiah Yeshua.

Finally, I want to acknowledge the guidance and encouragement throughout this project of God's Holy Spirit. His work in human hearts is the only hope of spiritual harmony for Jewish-Gentile couples or anyone else.

Tuvya Zaretsky
March 2016